simply shetland 2

at jack london ranch

"I ride over my beautiful ranch. Between my legs is a beautiful horse. The air is wine. The grapes on a score of rolling hills are red with autumn flame. Across Sonoma Mountain wisps of sea fog are stealing. The afternoon sun smolders in the drowsy sky. I have everything to make me glad I am alive."

—Jack London

foreword

What could be a better setting to showcase our second book of handknitting patterns than the place writer Jack London called Beauty Ranch? Set in the Sonoma Mountains near Glen Ellen, the ranch is every bit the unspoiled paradise today as it was in 1905 when London began acquiring the land.

On these pages, our designers make full use of the Shetland palette—more colors in more combinations than ever before. This season, we introduce two yarns. **Shetland Heather** aran weight yarn replaces Soft Shetland with a larger and more encompassing color spectrum. We've retained old favorites and added some wonderful new shades. Lace knitters will be pleased to see Sandi Rosner's **Marguerite Beaded Shawl** using the new **Shetland Ultra** lace yarn, a smooth blend of pure Shetland wool and lambswool.

We're pleased to offer this new collection. There are designs for all tastes and styles—projects for all levels of knitters. Whether you choose the simplicity of **Jack's Mittens** or the **Tivoli Scarf**, Hazel Hughson's classic **Gerda & Kai Pullovers**, Carol Lapin's challenging **Glen Ellen Jacket**, or the sheer whimsy of Nicky Epstein's **Autumn Leaves Felted Bag**, we're sure you'll enjoy the results of your efforts for years to come.

sonoma mountain wrap

carol lapin

MATERIALS

YARN: Jamieson's Shetland Double Knitting - 150 grams of Shetland Black (101); 75 grams each of Bracken (231); Burnt Umber (1190); Osprey (238); and Oxford (123); 50 grams each of Mogit (107); Moorit (108); Purple Haze (1270); Purple Heather (239); Seaweed (253); Spagnum (233); Sunrise (187); and Thistledown (237); 25 grams each of Olive (825); Peat (198); and Shaela (102).

NEEDLES: US 9 (5.5 mm) and US 11 (8 mm), *or correct needles to obtain gauge.* 2 mm and 3 mm crochet hook.

MEASUREMENTS
WIDTH: 25½". **LENGTH:** 88".

GAUGE
On US 11 in **Woven Stitch:** 22 sts and 30 rows = 4".

WOVEN STITCH (EVEN NO. OF STS) (SLIP ALL STS PWISE)

Row 1 (RS): K1; *sl 1 wyif, k1; rep from *; end sl 1 wyif.

Row 2 (WS): *P1; sl 1 wyib, p1; rep from *; end sl 1 wyib.

Rep these 2 rows. Always change color on Row 1 of **Woven Stitch**.

SHAWL

With US 11 and Shetland Black, CO 140 sts. Work

Stripe Sequence in **Woven Stitch**. With US 9, BO.

FINISHING

With Shetland Black and 2 mm crochet hook, work single crochet around entire edge of garment. With 3 mm crochet hook, work 2 double crochets in each single crochet around entire edge of garment, working 4 double crochets in each corner. Weave in ends. Block gently.

STRIPE SEQUENCE

8 rows Shetland Black
12 rows Mogit
8 rows Purple Heather
4 rows Bracken
20 rows Oxford
8 rows Osprey
4 rows Spagnum
6 rows Sunrise
6 rows Shaela
6 rows Moorit
4 rows Seaweed
8 rows Shetland Black
6 rows Thistledown
14 rows Burnt Umber
4 rows Osprey
6 rows Purple Heather
4 rows Peat
8 rows Oxford
4 rows Olive
8 rows Seaweed
6 rows Bracken
6 rows Mogit
8 rows Shetland Black
14 rows Burnt Umber
6 rows Sunrise
6 rows Purple Heather
8 rows Purple Haze
6 rows Spagnum
6 rows Oxford
6 rows Moorit
6 rows Osprey
8 rows Thistledown
6 rows Shetland Black
4 rows Olive
6 rows Seaweed
8 rows Burnt Umber
4 rows Bracken
10 rows Purple Heather
8 rows Purple Haze
6 rows Oxford
12 rows Osprey
8 rows Spagnum
6 rows Moorit

10 rows Shetland Black
8 rows Thistledown
6 rows Peat
6 rows Sunrise
10 rows Burnt Umber
6 rows Purple Haze
4 rows Seaweed
2 rows Bracken
14 rows Oxford
6 rows Osprey
4 rows Olive
4 rows Spagnum
4 rows Bracken
12 rows Moorit
8 rows Mogit
6 rows Purple Heather
4 rows Sunrise
12 rows Shetland Black
4 rows Bracken
10 rows Burnt Umber
8 rows Osprey
6 rows Seaweed
4 rows Purple Haze
16 rows Oxford
8 rows Peat
10 rows Thistledown
4 rows Seaweed
2 rows Bracken
8 rows Spagnum
8 rows Moorit
14 rows Sunrise
8 rows Burnt Umber
10 rows Purple Haze
10 rows Shetland Black
6 rows Shaela
10 rows Olive
16 rows Osprey
8 rows Purple Heather
4 rows Peat
12 rows Mogit
8 rows Bracken
6 rows Sunrise
16 rows Oxford
8 rows Burnt Umber

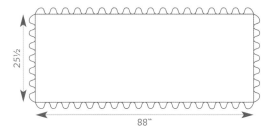

25½

88"

stripes! stripes! stripes!

beatrice smith

MATERIALS
(CHILD'S AMOUNTS IN PARENTHESES)
[ADULT'S AMOUNTS IN BRACKETS]

YARN: Jamieson's Shetland Double Knitting - (50, 50, 75) [75, 100, 125, 125] grams of Color A; (50, 50, 75) [75, 100, 125, 125] grams of Color B; (50, 50, 75) [75, 100, 125, 125] grams of Color C; (50, 50, 75) [75, 100, 125, 125] grams of Color D; (50, 50, 75) [75, 100, 125, 125] grams of Color E.
Child's version shown in Color A, Clyde Blue (168); Color B, Madder (587); Color C, Granny Smith (1140); Color D, Admiral Navy (727); and Color E, Daffodil (390).
Woman's version shown in Color A, Mulberry (598); Color B, Nighthawk (1020); Color C, Raspberry (1260); Color D, Sapphire (676); and Color E, Aubretia (1300).
Man's version shown in Color A, Clyde Blue (168); Color B, Rust (578); Color C, Shetland Black (101); Color D, Yellow Ochre (230); and Color E, Coffee (880).
NEEDLES: US 3 (3.25 mm) and US 5 (3.75 mm), *or correct needles to obtain gauge.*
ACCESSORIES: Stitch holders.

MEASUREMENTS
(CHILD'S SIZES IN PARENTHESES)
[ADULT'S SIZES IN BRACKETS]

CHEST: (28, 32, 36) [40, 44, 48, 52]".
LENGTH TO ARMHOLE: (10½, 13, 14) [14, 14, 14½, 15]".
ARMHOLE DEPTH: (6½, 7, 9) [10, 11, 11½, 12]".
LENGTH: (17, 20, 23) [24, 25, 26, 27]".
SLEEVE LENGTH TO UNDERARM: (12½, 15½, 17½) [18, 18½, 19, 20]".

GAUGE
On US 5 in st st: 21 sts and 32 rows = 4".

2X2 RIB PATTERN (MULTIPLE OF 4 + 2)
Row 1 (WS): P2; *k2, p2; rep from *.
Row 2 (RS): K2; *p2, k2; rep from *.

Rep Rows 1-2.

2X2 RIB PATTERN FOR NECKBAND (MULTIPLE OF 4)
Every Rnd: *K2, p2; rep from *.

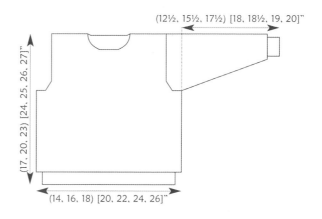

STRIPE SEQUENCE (ALL SIZES, ALL COLORWAYS)
*3 rows Color A, 7 rows Color B, 3 rows Color C, 7 rows Color D, 3 rows Color E, 7 rows Color A, 3 rows Color B, 7 rows Color C, 3 rows Color D, 7 rows Color E; rep from *.

BACK
With US 3 and Color A, CO (66, 78, 86) [94, 102, 110, 118] sts. Beg **Stripe Sequence** and work in **2X2 Rib Pattern** until piece measures (1½, 1½, 2) [2½, 3, 3, 3]" from CO edge, ending with RS facing for next row. Change to US 5 and st st, and continuing in **Stripe Sequence** throughout, inc (6, 6, 8) [10, 14, 16, 18] sts evenly spaced across row ((72, 84, 94) [104, 116, 126, 136] sts on needle). Continue in **Stripe Sequence** and st st until piece measures (10½, 13, 14) [14, 14, 14½, 15]" from CO edge, ending with RS facing for next row.

SHAPE ARMHOLES
BO (5, 5, 5) [5, 5, 5, 5] sts at beg of next 2 rows, then dec 1 st at beg and end of every RS row (3, 3, 3) [4, 5, 6, 7] times as follows: k2, k2tog; work to last 4 sts; ssk, k2. Work without further shaping on rem (56, 68, 78) [86, 96, 104, 112] sts until armhole measures 6 (6½, 8½) [9½, 10½, 11, 11½]", ending with RS facing for next row.

SHAPE BACK NECK

Next Row (RS): Knit (15, 20, 23) [26, 30, 32, 36] sts; knit (26, 28, 32) [34, 36, 40, 40] sts and place on holder for back neck; knit (15, 20, 23) [26, 30, 32, 36] sts.

Turn, and working each side separately, work 3 more rows, dec'g (1, 1, 1) [1, 1, 1, 1] st at neck edge on next RS row. Place rem (14, 19, 22) [25, 29, 31, 35] shoulder sts on holders.

FRONT

Work same as for back until armhole measures (4½, 5, 6½) [7½, 8, 8½, 9]", ending with RS facing for next row.

SHAPE FRONT NECK

Next Row (RS): Knit (23, 29, 33) [36, 41, 44, 48] sts; knit (10, 10, 12) [14, 14, 16, 16] sts and place on holder for front neck; knit (23, 29, 33) [36, 41, 44, 48] sts.

Turn, and working each side separately, BO 3 sts on every RS row (1, 2, 2) [2, 2, 2, 2] time(s), 2 sts (2, 1, 1) [1, 1, 2, 2] time(s), then dec 1 st at neck edge on every RS row (2, 2, 3) [3, 4, 3, 3] times. Continue without further shaping on rem (14, 19, 22) [25, 29, 31, 35] sts until piece measures same length as back. Place shoulder sts on holders.

JOIN SHOULDERS

Join shoulders using 3-needle bind-off method.

SLEEVES

With US 3 and Color A, CO (42, 46, 46) [50, 58, 58, 58] sts. Beg **Stripe Sequence** and work in **2X2 Rib Pattern** until piece measures (1½, 1½, 2) [2½, 3, 3, 3]" from CO edge, ending with RS facing for next row. Change to US 5 and st st, and continuing in **Stripe Sequence** throughout, inc (4, 4, 4) [6, 6, 6, 10] sts evenly spaced across row ((46, 50, 50) [56, 64, 64, 68] sts on needle).

Continue in **Stripe Sequence** and st st, **AND AT SAME TIME**, inc 1 st at beg and end of every 4th row (5, 0, 19) [28, 28, 30, 31] times, then every 6th row (10, 16, 6) [0, 0, 0, 0] times ((76, 82, 100) [112, 120, 124, 130] sts on needle). Work without further shaping until piece measures (12½ 15½, 17½) [18, 18½, 19, 20]" from CO edge.

SHAPE SLEEVE CAP

BO (5, 5, 5) [5, 5, 5, 5] sts at beg of next 2 rows, then dec 1 st at beg and end of every RS row (3, 3, 3) [4, 5, 6, 7] times as follows: k2, k2tog; work to last 4 sts; ssk, k2. BO rem (60, 66, 84) [94, 100, 102, 106] sts on next row.

NECKBAND

With US 3 and next color in **Stripe Sequence** from those on holder for front neck, beg at right shoulder seam, pick up (3, 3, 3) [3, 3, 3, 3] sts to back neck holder, knit (26, 28, 32) [34, 36, 40, 40] sts from back neck holder, pick up (3, 3, 3) [3, 3, 3, 3] sts to left shoulder seam, pick up (17, 18, 21) [21, 24, 25, 25] sts down left neck edge, knit (10, 10, 12) [14, 14, 16, 16] sts from front neck holder, pick up (17, 18, 21) [21, 24, 25, 25] up right neck edge ((76, 80, 92) [96, 104, 112, 112] sts on needle). Work in **2X2 Rib Pattern for Neckband**, continuing in **Stripe Sequence** as set, until neckband measures (1, 1, 1¼) [1¼, 1½, 1½, 1½]". BO in pattern.

FINISHING

Sew sleeves to body. Sew side and sleeve seams. Weave in ends. Block to finished measurements.

gerda & kai pullovers

hazel hughson

MATERIALS

YARN: Jamieson's Shetland 2-Ply Spindrift - *Gerda Colorway:* 25 (50, 50, 50) grams of Caspian (760); 25 (50, 50, 50) grams of Cloud (764); 125 (150, 175, 225) grams of Granite (122); 125 (150, 175, 225) grams of Natural White (104); 25 (25, 25, 25) grams of Mint (770); 50 (75, 75, 100) grams of Seabright (1010); 25 (50, 50, 75) grams of Surf (135); and 25 (25, 25, 50) grams of Teviot (136). *Kai Colorway:* 25 (25, 25, 50) grams of Atlantic (150); 25 (50, 50, 50) grams of Highland Mist (1390); 125 (150, 175, 225) grams of Moorland (195); 25 (50, 50, 50) grams of Nighthawk (1020); 125 (150, 175, 225) grams of Osprey (238); 25 (25, 25, 25) grams of Purple Heather (239); 50 (75, 75, 100) grams of Stonewash (677); and 25 (50, 50, 75) grams of Twilight (175).
NEEDLES: Circular and/or double-pointed US 2 (3 mm) and US 3 (3.25 mm), *or correct needles to obtain gauge.*
ACCESSORIES: Stitch holders. Tapestry needle (for finishing).

MEASUREMENTS

CHEST: 36 (42, 48, 54)".
LENGTH TO ARMHOLE: 14½ (15, 15½, 16)".
ARMHOLE DEPTH: 9½ (10, 10½, 11)".
LENGTH: 24 (25, 26, 27)".
SLEEVE LENGTH: 17 (18, 19, 19)".

GAUGE

On US 3 in **Chart B**: 32 sts and 32 rows = 4".

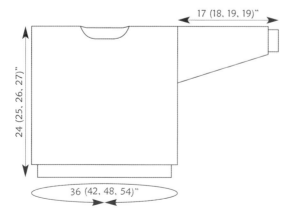

ABOUT CHARTS

As garment is knit entirely in the rnd, read all rows from right to left. Knit all sts in Chart B. Be sure to read special instructions printed below Charts A and C.

BODY

With US 2 and Granite, (Gerda Colorway) **OR** Moorland (Kai Colorway), CO 260 (300, 344, 388) sts. Place marker, join and work the 23 rows of **Chart A** for your colorway.

Change to US 3 and work 2 rnds in Granite (Gerda Colorway) **OR** Moorland (Kai Colorway), inc'g 28 (36, 40, 44) sts evenly spaced in 1st rnd (288 (336, 384, 432) sts on needle).

Beg at points marked for your size, work **Chart B** for your colorway until piece measures 14½ (15, 15½, 16)" from CO edge.

SET ARMHOLE STEEKS

Next Rnd: Place 1st st of rnd on holder. With alt colors, CO 5 sts (1 edge st and 4 steek sts); mark 1st cast-on st for beg of rnd; continue **Chart B** for your colorway as set on next 143 (167, 191, 215) sts; place next st on holder; CO 10 sts (1 edge st on each side and 8 steek sts); continue **Chart B** for your colorway as set on next 143 (167, 191, 215) sts; with alt colors, CO 5 sts (1 edge st and 4 steek sts); place marker to indicate beg of rnd.

Working steek sts in alt colors and edge sts in background color, continue **Chart B** for your colorway as set until armhole measures 7 (7½, 7½, 8)".

SHAPE NECK

Next Rnd: Work 4 steek sts and 1 edge st; continue **Chart B** for your colorway as set on next 54 (66, 77, 89) sts; place next 35 (35, 37, 37) sts on holder for front neck. With alt colors, CO 10 sts (1 edge st on each side and 8 steek sts); continue **Chart B** for your colorway to end of rnd.

Continuing **Chart B** for your colorway as set, dec 1 st at each side of neck steek on next 4 (4, 4, 4) rnds, then

Gerda Chart B

Gerda Chart A

Note on Chart A:
With color indicated, knit sts 1-2 and purl sts 3-4.

Gerda Color Key

✖	Caspian (760)
•	Cloud (764)
◇	Granite (122)
☐	Natural White (104)
–	Mint (770)
▨	Seabright (1010)
○	Surf (135)
▊	Teviot (136)

Gerda Chart B (Cont'd)

Gerda Chart C

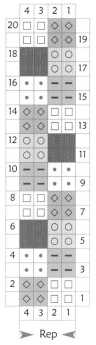

Note on Chart C:
With color indicated, purl odd-numbered rnds and knit even-numbered rnds.

Gerda Color Key

✕	Caspian (760)
•	Cloud (764)
◇	Granite (122)
□	Natural White (104)
—	Mint (770)
▪	Seabright (1010)
○	Surf (135)
▪	Teviot (136)

every alt rnd 6 (6, 7, 7) times (44 (56, 66, 78) sts rem for each shoulder). **AT SAME TIME**, when armhole measures 8½ 9, 9½ 10)", shape back neck as follows: work 48 (60, 70, 82) sts from right shoulder steek, place 47 (47, 51, 51) sts on holder for back neck, CO 10 sts (1 edge st on each side and 8 steek sts); work 48 (60, 70, 82) sts to left shoulder steek, dec 1 (1, 1, 1) st at neck edge on next rnd, then every alt rnd 3 (3, 3, 3) times (44 (56, 66, 78) sts rem for each shoulder).

JOIN SHOULDERS
With background color for your colorway, join shoulders using 3-needle bind-off method (or weave with kitchener st, if desired).

SLEEVES
Cut sleeve steeks open through center st (between 4th and 5th sts) and back stitch up center of 1st and last steek sts. Place st from holder onto US 3 circular or double-pointed needle and mark this st as beg of rnd. With Granite (Gerda Colorway) **OR** Moorland (Kai Colorway), pick up 152 (160, 168, 176) sts between edge st and steek st evenly around armhole. Turning **Chart B** for your colorway upside down and working backwards through chart, beg at points marked for your size, and working the marked st in background color throughout, work 4 (4, 4, 4) rnds, then continue backwards through chart, **AND AT SAME TIME**, dec 1 st on each side of marked st every 3rd rnd 20 (24, 27, 24) times, then every 2nd rnd 20 (19, 19, 25) times (72 (74, 76, 78) sts rem). Continue without further shaping until sleeve measures 14 (15, 16, 16)".

DEC FOR CUFF
Next Rnd: With Granite (Gerda Colorway) **OR** Moorland (Kai Colorway), work in st st for 1 rnd, dec'g 12 (14, 12, 14) sts evenly around (60 (60, 64, 64) sts on needle). Change to US 2, turn **Chart A** upside down and work backwards through chart. BO.

FINISHING
Secure 1st and last st of front neck steek. Cut steek through center st.

NECKBAND
GERDA COLORWAY
With US 2 and Granite, pick up 5 (5, 5, 5) sts from right shoulder seam to back neck holder; knit the 47 (47, 51, 51) sts from back neck holder; pick up 5 (5, 5, 5) sts to left shoulder seam; pick up 16 (16, 17, 17) sts down left front neck edge; knit the 35 (35, 37, 37) sts from front neck holder; pick up 16 (16, 17, 17) sts up right front neck edge (124 (124, 132, 132) sts on needle). Work **Chart C for Gerda Colorway**. With Granite, knit facing as follows:

Next Rnd: With Granite knit.
Next Rnd (Turning Rnd): With Granite, purl.

With Granite, knit approx. 20 rnds for facing (facing should equal length of neckband). BO.

Fold facing at turning rnd and sew to inside.

KAI COLORWAY
With US 2 and Moorland, pick up 5 (5, 5, 5) sts from right shoulder seam to back neck holder; knit the 47 (47, 51, 51) sts from back neck holder; pick up 5 (5, 5, 5) sts to left shoulder seam; pick up 16 (16, 17, 17) sts down left front neck edge; knit the 35 (35, 37, 37) sts from front neck holder; pick up 16 (16, 17, 17) sts up right front neck edge (124 (124, 132, 132) sts on needle). Work **Chart C for Kai Colorway**. BO.

Trim all steeks and cross stitch in place. Weave in ends. Block to finished measurements.

Kai Chart B

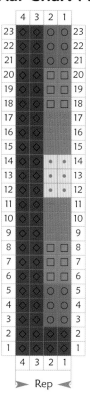

Kai Chart A

Note on Chart A: With color indicated, knit sts 1-2 and purl sts 3-4.

Kai Color Key

- Atlantic (150)
- Highland Mist (1390)
- Moorland (195)
- Nighthawk (1020)
- Osprey (238)
- Purple Heather (239)
- Stonewash (677)
- Twilight (175)

Kai Chart B (Cont'd)

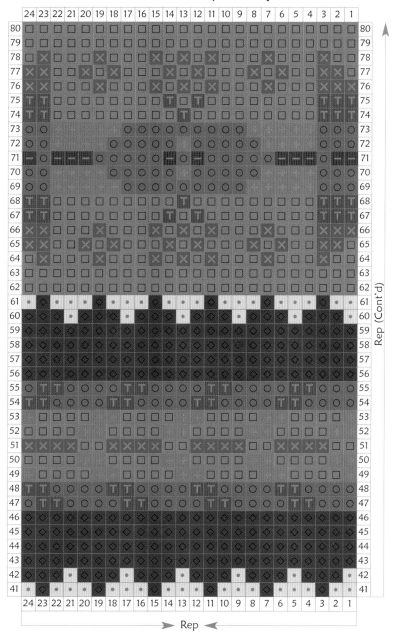

Kai Chart C

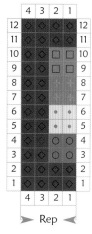

Note on Chart C: With color indicated, knit sts 1-2 and purl sts 3-4.

Kai Color Key

- Atlantic (150)
- Highland Mist (1390)
- Moorland (195)
- Nighthawk (1020)
- Osprey (238)
- Purple Heather (239)
- Stonewash (677)
- Twilight (175)

elsinore pullover

gregory courtney

MATERIALS
YARN: Jamieson's Shetland Double Knitting - 225 (325) grams. Shown in Emerald (792) and Plum (585).
NEEDLES: 16" and 32" circular US 4 (3.50 mm) and 32" US 5 (3.75 mm), *or correct needles to obtain gauge*.
ACCESSORIES: Stitch holders.

MEASUREMENTS
CHEST: 27½ (33)".
LENGTH: 17 (21)".
SLEEVE LENGTH: 13 (15½)".

GAUGE
On US 5 in **Chart**: 28 sts and 32 rows = 4".

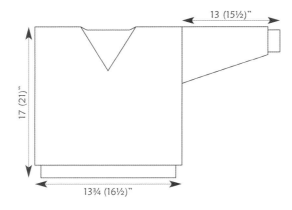

13 (15½)"

17 (21)"

13¾ (16½)"

NOTES ON CHART
Read odd-numbered (RS) rows from right to left and even-numbered (WS) rows from left to right.

BACK
With US 4, CO 86 (102) sts. Beg and ending at points marked for your size, work **Foundation Row**, **Ribbing** and **Increase Row** of **Chart**, then change to US 5 and rep Rows 1-16 until piece measures 16½ (20½)" from CO edge, ending with RS facing for next row.

SHAPE BACK NECK
Next Row (RS): Work 30 (38) sts, work next 36 (38) sts and place on holder for back neck, work 30 (38) sts.

Turn, and working each side separately, work 3 more rows (last row is a WS row). Place rem 30 (38) shoulder sts on holders.

FRONT
Work same as for back until piece measures 11½ (14½)" from CO edge, ending with RS facing for next row.

SHAPE FRONT NECK
Next Row (RS): Work 47 (56) sts, work next 2 sts and place on holder, work 47 (56) sts.

Turn, and working each side separately, dec 1 st at neck edge every 2nd row 17 (18) times. Work without further shaping on rem 30 (38) sts until piece measures same length as back, ending after working a WS row.

JOIN SHOULDERS
Join shoulders using 3-needle bind-off method.

SLEEVES
With US 4, CO 38 (38) sts. Beg and ending at points marked for your size, work **Foundation Row**, **Ribbing** and **Increase Row** of **Chart**, then change to US 5 and rep Rows 1-16, **AND AT SAME TIME**, inc 1 st at beg and end of next row, then every 2nd row 5 (0) times, then every 4th row 18 (27) times, working inc'd sts into background st (90 (98) sts on needle). Continue without further shaping until sleeve measures 13 (15½)" from CO edge. BO.

NECKBAND
With 16" circular US 4, beg at right shoulder seam, pick up 5 (5) sts from right shoulder seam to back neck holder, k36 (38) from back neck holder, pick up 5 (5) sts to left shoulder seam, pick up 38 (46) sts down left neck edge, place marker, k2 from holder, pick up 38 (46) sts up right neck edge (124 (142) sts on needle). Join, and work in the rnd as follows:

Every Rnd: Work k2, p2 rib to 2 sts before marker, work 2 sts tog (dec), slip marker, k2, slip marker, work 2 sts tog (dec), continue rib as set to end of rnd.

Rep this rnd until neckband measures 7/8". BO in pattern.

FINISHING
Center sleeves on shoulder seams and sew into place. Weave in ends. Block to finished measurements.

Chart

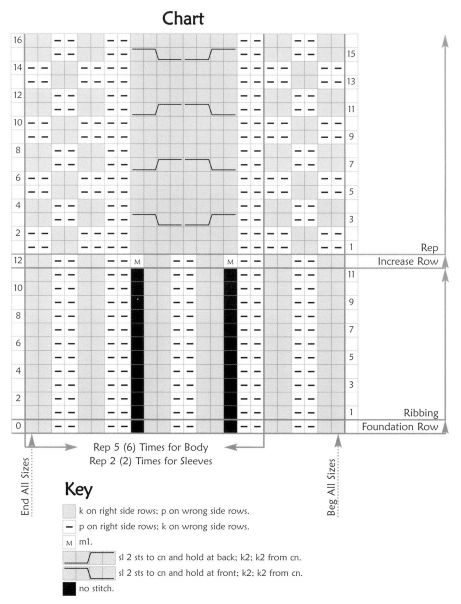

Rep
Increase Row
Ribbing
Foundation Row

Rep 5 (6) Times for Body
Rep 2 (2) Times for Sleeves

End All Sizes

Beg. All Sizes

Key

k on right side rows; p on wrong side rows.

— p on right side rows; k on wrong side rows.

M m1.

sl 2 sts to cn and hold at back; k2; k2 from cn.

sl 2 sts to cn and hold at front; k2; k2 from cn.

no stitch.

glen ellen jacket

carol lapin

MATERIALS

YARN: Jamieson's Shetland Double Knitting - 75 (100) grams each of Atlantic (150); Bracken (231); Eucalyptus (794); Pine (234); Rosemary (821); Sage (766); Seaweed (253); and Spagnum (233). 50 (50) grams of Clover (596).
NEEDLES: US 4 (3.50 mm) and US 6 (4 mm), *or correct needles to obtain gauge*.
ACCESSORIES: Stitch holders. Five ¾" buttons.

MEASUREMENTS

CHEST: 44 (52)".
LENGTH: 27½ (27½)".
SLEEVE LENGTH: 19 (19)".

GAUGE

On US 7 in **Chevron Stitch**: 31 sts and 29 rows = 4".

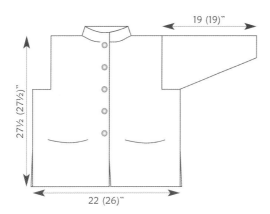

CHEVRON STITCH (MULTIPLE OF 14 + 3)

Note: The number of sts changes from Row 1 to Row 2. Slip all sts pwise.
Row 1 (RS): K1, sl 1, k1, psso, *k11, sl 2, k1, p2sso; rep from * to last 14 sts; end k11, k2tog, k1.
Row 2 (WS): K1, *p1, k5 ([k1, yo, k1] in next st), k5; rep from * to last 2 sts; end p1, k1

Rep Rows 1 and 2.

COLOR SEQUENCE

*Work 8 rows each of Atlantic, Pine, Spagnum, Bracken, Seaweed, Sage, Eucalyptus, and Rosemary; rep from * throughout.

BACK

With US 6 and Atlantic, CO 171 (199) sts. Working in **Chevron Stitch** throughout, work 2 reps of **Color Sequence,** ending after working 4th row in Rosemary. Work will measure approximately 17 (17)" with RS facing for next row.

SHAPE ARMHOLES

Next Row (RS) (5th Row of Rosemary): K1, sl 1, k1, psso, k5, k2tog, k11, k2tog, k5, sl 2, k1, p2sso; continue in pattern as set until 23 sts rem; k2tog, k11, k2tog, k5, k2tog, k1.

Next Row (WS) (6th Row of Rosemary): K1, p1, k23, p1; continue in pattern as set until 25 sts rem; k23, p1, k1.

Next Row (RS) (7th Row of Rosemary): K1, sl 1, k1, psso, k21, sl 2, k1, p2sso; continue in pattern until 24 sts rem; k21, k2tog, k1.

Next Row (WS) (8th Row of Rosemary): K1, p1, k21, p1; continue in pattern as set until 23 sts rem; k21, p1, k1.

Next Row (RS): BO 20 sts. Attach Atlantic and BO 1 st; sl2, k1, p2sso; continue with Atlantic in pattern st as set until 25 sts rem; k2tog, k1; with Rosemary, BO rem 22 sts.

Note: *From this point on, there will be 99 (123) sts on needle after Row 1 of* **Chevron Stitch** *and 115 (143) sts on needle after Row 2 of* **Chevron Stitch.**
Continue in **Color Sequence,** ending after working 8 rows in Rosemary.

SHAPE BACK NECK

Row 1 (RS): With Atlantic, work 30 (44) sts, dec 5 (7) sts evenly across (25 (37) sts rem). Turn.
Row 2 (WS): Knit.
Row 3 (RS): Knit.
Row 4 (WS): Knit.

Place shoulder sts on holder. Place 55 (55) center sts on another holder for back neck. Work Rows 1-4 above for left shoulder. Place shoulder sts on holder.

MAKE POCKET LININGS (MAKE 2)
With US 4 and Clover, CO 45 (45) sts.

Row 1 (RS): K1, sl 1, k1, psso, ([k11, sl 2, k1, p2sso] twice); end k11, k2tog, k1 (39 sts on needle).
Row 2 (WS): P7 *([p1, yo, p1] in next st), p11; rep from * to last 8 sts; p1, yo, p1 in next st; end p7.

Rep Rows 1-2 above until pocket lining measures 4½ (4½)". Place on holder.

LEFT FRONT
With US 6 and Atlantic, CO 87 (101) sts. Working in **Chevron Stitch** throughout, work 1 rep of **Color Sequence**, ending after working 7th row of Rosemary.

Next Row (WS) (8th Row of Rosemary): Work 28 (28) sts in pattern as set, BO next 39 (39) sts for pocket opening, work 14 (28) sts in pattern as set.

INSERT POCKET LININGS
NEXT ROW (RS): With Atlantic, work 14 (28) sts in pattern as set, place pocket sts on left-hand needle and work in pattern; work last 28 (28) sts in pattern.

Continue in **Chevron Stitch** and **Color Sequence** until piece measures approximately 17 (17)" from CO edge, ending after working 4 rows in Rosemary, with RS facing for next row.

SHAPE ARMHOLE
Next Row (RS) (5th Row of Rosemary): K1, sl 1, k1, psso, k5, k2tog, k11, k2tog, k5, sl 2, k1, p2sso; continue in pattern to end of row.
Next Row (WS) (6th Row of Rosemary): K1, p1, k23, p1; continue in pattern to end of row.
Next Row (RS) (7th Row of Rosemary): K1, sl 1, k1, psso, k21, sl 2, k1, p2sso; continue in pattern to end of row.
Next Row (WS) (8th Row of Rosemary): K1, p1, k21, p1; continue in pattern to end of row.

Continue in **Chevron Stitch** and **Color Sequence** through Sage.

SHAPE NECK
Next Row (RS) (1st Row of Eucalyptus): Work in pattern until 14 (14) sts rem; place these on holder.

Continuing in **Chevron Stitch** and **Color Sequence**, dec 1 st at neck edge on every row until 30 (44) sts rem, counting sts after completing Row 2 of **Chevron Stitch**. *Do not work k1, yo, k1 in next st as in first rep of Row 2.* Work in pattern on these 30 (44) sts until all 8 rows of Rosemary have been completed. Change to Atlantic and work knit 30 (44) sts, dec'g 5 (7) sts evenly spaced across row. Knit next 3 rows. Place rem 25 (37) sts on holder for left shoulder.

RIGHT FRONT
With US 6 and Atlantic, CO 87 (101) sts. Working in **Chevron Stitch** throughout, work 1 rep of **Color Sequence**, ending after working 7th row of Rosemary.

Next Row (WS) (8th row of Rosemary): Work 14 (28) sts in pattern as set, BO next 39 (39) sts for pocket opening, work 28 (28) sts in pattern as set.

INSERT POCKET LININGS
Next Row (RS): With Atlantic, work 28 (28) sts in pattern as set, place pocket sts on left-hand needle and work in pattern; work last 14 (28) sts in pattern as set.

Continue in **Chevron Stitch** and **Color Sequence** through 4th row of 2nd occurrence of Pine.

MAKE 1ST BUTTONHOLE

Next Row (RS) (5th row of Pine): K1, sl 1, k1, psso, k5, yo, k2tog, k4, sl 2, k1, p2sso; continue in pattern to end of row.

Continue in **Chevron Stitch** and **Color Sequence**, making 2nd buttonhole in 5th row of Seaweed, 3rd buttonhole in 5th row of Atlantic, 4th buttonhole in 5th row of Spagnum, and 5th buttonhole in 5th row of Sage, working buttonhole row same as for 1st buttonhole.

Continue in **Chevron Stitch** and **Color Sequence** through Sage.

SHAPE NECK

Next Row (RS) (1st Row of Eucalyptus): Work first 14 (14) sts in pattern and place on holder; work rem sts in pattern.

Continuing in **Chevron Stitch** and **Color Sequence**, dec 1 st at neck edge on every row until 30 (44) sts rem, counting sts after completing Row 2 of **Chevron Stitch**. *On row 2, in first rep of pattern only, do not work k1, yo, k1 incs.*

Row 1 (RS): On first rep of pattern only, k2tog, k11, sl 2, k1, p2sso; work in pattern to end of row.
Row 2 (WS): Work in pattern to last rep; end k6.

Rep these 2 rows until 8 rows of Rosemary have been completed. Change to Atlantic and k30 (44) sts, dec'g 5 (7) sts evenly spaced across row. Knit next 3 rows. Place rem 25 (37) sts on holder for right shoulder.`

JOIN SHOULDERS

Join shoulders using 3-needle bind-off-method.

NECKBAND

With US 4, RS facing, slip 14 (14) sts from right front holder onto needle (don't knit them). With Atlantic, pick up 30 (30) sts along neck edge to back neck holder. Break yarn. Slip next 55 (55) sts from back neck holder onto needle (don't knit them). Attach Atlantic and pick up 30 (30) sts down left neck edge to front neck holder. Slip 14 (14) sts from left front neck holder onto needle (don't knit them) (143 (143) sts on needle). Break yarn and re-attach with RS facing. Work in **Chevron Stitch**, continuing **Color Sequence** as set until 8 rows of Spagnum are complete. BO.

SLEEVES

Notes: *Because st count changes from Row 1 to Row 2 in* **Chevron Stitch***, it is best to isolate first and last pattern rep with markers and always keep st count the same on Row 1 and 2 until it is time to dec (every 6th row). Sometimes, you will have to work a double decrease or a double increase to make this happen. You will be decreasing 1½ pattern reps on each side of the sleeve.*

With US 6 and Atlantic, pick up 71 (71) sts from underarm to shoulder seam, pick up 1 (1) st in shoulder seam, pick up 71 (71) sts down to underarm (143 (143) sts on needle). Work **Chevron Stitch** in **Color Sequence** (in reverse order). After 2 stripes, beg decs as follows: dec 1 st at beg and end of every 6th row (3 garter ridges) until approx 93 (93) sts rem after Row 2 of pattern stitch. With US 4, work last stripe (Atlantic). BO.

FINISHING

Sew sleeve seams. Sew side seams leaving approximately 6½ (6½)" open at bottom. Sew buttons opposite buttonholes. Block to finished measurements.

jack's mittens

gregory courtney

MATERIALS

YARN: Jamieson's Shetland Chunky Marl (or Chunky Shetland) - 100 grams. Shown in Harvest (2101) and Merlot (2103).
NEEDLES: Set of 5 double-pointed US 8 (5 mm), *or correct needles to obtain gauge*.
ACCESSORIES: Tapestry needle (for finishing).

MEASUREMENTS
LENGTH: 10½".
CIRCUMFERENCE AT PALM: 9".

GAUGE
On US 8 in st st: 16 sts and 23 rows = 4".

DESIGNER NOTES

There is no right- or left-hand mitten—knit both alike. They're knitted on smaller needles than usual for chunky weight yarn and will feel somewhat stiff. Hand wash gently—the wool will bloom and soften and the mittens will be warm and a pleasure to wear.

CUFF

With US 8, CO 36 sts. Divide onto 4 needles, join and work in k2, p2 ribbing for 3".

SHAPE THUMB GUSSET

Change to st st and work as follows:

Rnd 1: K18, place marker, m1, place marker, knit to end of rnd.
Rnds 2, 4, 6, 7, 9, 10, 12, 13 & 14: Knit.
Rnds 3, 5, 8, 11 & 15: Knit to first marker, slip marker, m1, knit to 2nd marker, m1, slip marker, knit to end of rnd.

Next Rnd: Knit to 1st marker, remove marker, slip 11 thumb sts onto scrap piece of yarn, remove marker, CO 1, knit to end of rnd (37 sts on needles).

Continue in st st until mitten measures 8½" from CO edge, dec'g 1 st on last row.

SHAPE TOP

Dec Rnd: *1st Needle:* k1, ssk, knit to end of needle; *2nd Needle:* knit to last 3 sts, k2tog, k1; *3rd Needle:* k1, ssk, knit to end of needle; *4th Needle:* knit to last 3 sts, k2tog, k1.

Continue in st st, working **Dec Rnd** every other rnd until there are 5 sts on each needle (20 in all), then work **Dec Rnd** every rnd until 2 sts rem on each needle (8 in all). Break yarn, leaving about a 4" tail. Thread onto tapestry needle, draw through rem sts and push thread through hole to inside of mitten. Pull tight to close hole. Weave in end.

THUMB

Divide thumb sts onto 3 needles. Reattach yarn and knit first rnd, picking up 1 st at end of rnd to bridge gap between thumb and hand (12 sts on needles). Work in st st for 2¾".

Next Rnd: K2tog 6 times.

Break yarn and close hole same as for top of mitten.

FINISHING

Weave in ends. Hand wash gently and lay flat to dry.

aurora kimono

carol lapin

MATERIALS

YARN: Jamieson's 2-ply Shetland Spindrift - 425 grams of Color A; 300 grams of Color B; and 50 grams of Color C.
Shown in Color A, Spagnum (233); Color B, Black (999); and Color C, Maroon (595).
NEEDLES: 16", 20" and 32" circular US 3 (3.25 mm), 16" circular US 4 (3.5 mm) and two 32" circular US 5 (3.75 mm),
or correct needles to obtain gauge.
ACCESSORIES: Stitch holders.

MEASUREMENTS

CHEST: 46".
LENGTH TO ARMHOLE: 10".
ARMHOLE DEPTH: 15".
LENGTH: 25".
SLEEVE LENGTH: 16½".

GAUGE

On US 5 in **Honeycomb Stitch:** 29 sts and 46 rows = 4".

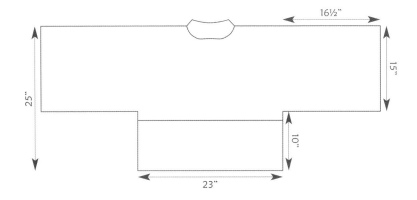

HONEYCOMB STITCH (MULTIPLE OF 8 + 4)

Row 1 (RS): With Color A, knit.
Row 2 (WS): With Color A. knit.
Rows 3, 5 & 7 (RS): With Color B, k1 (edge st); *sl 2 sts pwise wyib, k6; rep from * to last 3 sts; end sl 2 sts pwise wyib, k1 (edge st).
Rows 4, 6 & 8 (WS): With Color B, p1 (edge st); *sl 2 sts pwise wyif, p6; rep from * to last 3 sts; end sl 2 sts pwise wyif, p1 (edge st).
Row 9 (RS): With Color A, knit.
Row 10 (WS): With Color A, knit.
Rows 11, 13 & 15 (RS): With Color B, k1 (edge st), k4, sl 2 sts pwise wyib; *k6, sl 2 sts pwise wyib; rep from * to last 5 sts; end k4, k1 (edge st).
Rows 12, 14 & 16 (WS): With Color B, p1 (edge st), p4, sl 2 sts pwise wyif; *p6, sl 2 sts pwise wyif; rep from * to last 5 sts; end p4, p1 (edge st).

Rep Rows 1-16.

HONEYCOMB STITCH REVERSED (MULTIPLE OF 8 + 4)

Work same as for **Honeycomb Stitch**, working Color B in place of Color A, and Color A in place of Color B.

BACK BOTTOM PANEL

With US 5 and Color A, CO 164 sts. Knit 1 row. Work Rows 3-16 of **Honeycomb Stitch**, then rep Rows 1-16 until there are 5 reps. With Color A, knit 2 rows. With Color B, work in st st for 10 rows. Leave sts on needle and put aside.

BACK BODY

With another US 5 and Color B, CO 164 sts. Knit 1 row. Work Rows 3-16 of **Honeycomb Stitch Reversed**, then work Rows 1-8. Leave sts on needle.

JOIN BOTTOM PANEL TO BACK BODY

Hold needle with back bottom panel behind needle with back body, RS facing, and beg with Row 9 of **Honeycomb Stitch Reversed**, knit each st of back bottom panel tog with each st of back body. Continue through Row 16 of pattern.

CAST ON FOR SLEEVES

Continuing pattern as set, CO 112 sts at beg of next 2 rows (388 sts on needle). Continue as set until there are 13 reps of **Honeycomb Stitch Reversed**, then work Rows 1-8. With Color B, k169, BO next 50 sts for back neck, k169. Place shoulder sts on separate holders.

FRONT BOTTOM PANEL

Work same as for back bottom panel.

FRONT BODY

Work same as for back body until there 11 reps of **Honeycomb Stitch Reversed**, then work Rows 1-8.

Next Row (RS) (Row 9 of pattern): With Color B, knit 187 sts, BO next 14 sts for front neck, knit 187 sts.

Turn, and working each side separately and continuing pattern as set, BO 2 sts at neck edge 6 times, then dec 1 st at neck edge 6 times. Continue without further shaping on rem 169 sts until piece matches back, ending after working Row 9 of pattern with Color B. Place shoulder sts on separate holders.

FINISHING

With WS's facing and holding back piece toward you, join shoulders using 3-needle BO method.

NECKBAND

With US 4 and Color A, RS facing, beg at right shoulder seam, pick up 104 sts evenly around neck edge. Place marker, join, and with Color A, purl 1 rnd.

Rnds 1-6: With Color B, *sl 2 sts pwise, k6; rep from * to end of rnd.
Rnd 7: With Color A, knit. **Rnd 8:** With Color A, purl.
Rnds 9-14 : With Color B, k4, sl 2 sts pwise; *k6, sl 2 sts pwise; rep from * to last 4 sts; end k4.
Rnd 15: With Color A, knit. **Rnd 16:** With Color A, purl.

Work Rnds 1-16 again.

Change to US 3 and Color B and knit 24 rnds for neckband facing. BO. Turn to inside and sew down.

BOTTOM TRIM

With 32" US 3 and Color C, RS facing, pick up approx. 264 sts evenly around bottom edge, place marker, join and purl 4 rnds. BO.

SLEEVE TRIM

With 20" US 3 and Color C, RS facing, pick up approx. 180 sts evenly around sleeve cuff, place marker, join and purl 4 rnds. BO.

NECKBAND TRIM

With 16" US 3 and Color C, RS facing, pick up approx. 104 sts evenly around neckband opening, place marker, join and purl 1 rnd. BO.

Weave in ends. Block to finished measurements.

charmian capelet

carol lapin

MATERIALS

YARN: Jamieson's Shetland Double Knitting - 50 grams each of Blue Lovat (232); Burnt Umber (1190); Foxglove (273); Highland Mist (1390); Pacific (763); Purple Haze (1270); Purple Heather (239); Seaweed (253); Spagnum (233); and Thistledown (237).
NEEDLES: 16" and 32" circular US 6 (4 mm), *or correct needles to obtain gauge.*

MEASUREMENTS

LENGTH: 20" (measured from neck to point*****); 17" (measured from neck to straight edge*****)
*Not including **Neck Border** or **Bottom Border**.

GAUGE

On US 6 in st st: 22 sts and 31 rows = 4".

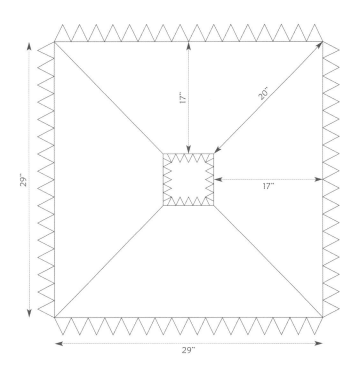

DESIGNER NOTE

Knit the capelet in the rnd from the top down.

BODY

With US 6 and Seaweed, CO 30 sts, place marker, CO 30 sts, place marker, CO 30 sts, place marker, CO 30 sts, place marker (use a different color marker here to indicate beg of rnd) (120 sts on needle). Join, and work in the rnd in st st following **Stripe Sequence for Body, AND AT SAME TIME**, inc 1 st before and after each marker (knit into back and front of st), every other rnd until there 160 sts between each marker (640 sts on needle). BO.

BOTTOM BORDER

With US 6 and Purple Heather (this is the first color in **Color Sequence for Bottom Border**), CO 2 sts.

* Row 1 (RS): Knit.
Row 2 (WS): Knit into front and back of first st, sl last st, and with WS of garment facing, beginning at any corner, pick up and knit 1 st from bottom edge, psso.
Row 3 (RS): Knit.
Row 4 (WS): Knit into front and back of first st, knit to last st, sl last st, and with WS of garment facing, pick up and knit 1 st from bottom edge, psso.

Rep Rows 3 and 4 until there are 7 sts on needle.

Row 1 (RS): Knit.
Row 2 (WS): K2tog, knit to last st, sl1, pick up and knit 1 st from edge, psso.

Rep Rows 1 and 2 above until 2 sts rem.****** Break yarn. With rem 2 sts on needle and next color in **Color Sequence for Bottom Border,** rep from ***** to ******, continuing color sequence for each point around bottom edge. *You'll make 16 triangles along bottom of each side—64 triangles total around bottom edge.*

NECK BORDER

Work same as for **Bottom Border**, working **Color Sequence for Neck Border** and working up to 5 sts instead

charmian capelet

of 7. *You'll make 5 triangles per side—20 triangles total around neck edge.*

FINISHING
Weave in ends. Block to finished measurements.

STRIPE SEQUENCE FOR BODY

5 rnds Seaweed	4 rnds Spagnum	2 rnds Pacific	2 rnds Foxglove
4 rnds Blue Lovat	2 rnds Purple Haze	5 rnds Seaweed	5 rnds Seaweed
2 rnds Purple Heather	3 rnds Highland Mist	2 rnds Highland Mist	2 rnds Purple Haze
5 rnds Thistledown	1 rnd Pacific	2 rnds Burnt Umber	3 rnds Highland Mist
2 rnds Highland Mist	2 rnds Purple Heather	4 rnds Purple Haze	3 rnds Purple Haze
3 rnds Burnt Umber	4 rnds Seaweed	3 rnds Blue Lovat	5 rnds Blue Lovat
6 rnds Seaweed	3 rnds Purple Haze	2 rnds Purple Heather	2 rnds Burnt Umber
2 rnds Pacific	2 rnds Burnt Umber	5 rnds Thistledown	5 rnds Thistledown
3 rnds Foxglove	4 rnds Thistledown	4 rnds Spagnum	2 rnds Purple Heather
5 rnds Thistledown	5 rnds Spagnum	2 rnds Pacific	
1 rnd Burnt Umber	3 rnds Foxglove	1 rnd Burnt Umber	

COLOR SEQUENCE FOR BOTTOM BORDER

Purple Heather	Foxglove	Foxglove	Blue Lovat
Burnt Umber	Burnt Umber	Highland Mist	Thistledown
Pacific	Spagnum	Spagnum	Spagnum
Purple Haze	Pacific	Purple Haze	Pacific
Blue Lovat	Highland Mist	Pacific	Foxglove
Spagnum	Purple Heather	Burnt Umber	Burnt Umber
Highland Mist	Blue Lovat	Purple Heather	Seaweed
Foxglove	Burnt Umber	Seaweed	Pacific
Thistledown	Foxglove	Highland Mist	Thistledown
Burnt Umber	Spagnum	Foxglove	Spagnum
Purple Haze	Highland Mist	Thistledown	Purple Heather
Spagnum	Purple Heather	Spagnum	Burnt Umber
Purple Heather	Pacific	Pacific	Blue Lovat
Pacific	Burnt Umber	Burnt Umber	Seaweed
Purple Haze	Thistledown	Purple Heather	Highland Mist
Highland Mist	Blue Lovat	Seaweed	Purple Haze

COLOR SEQUENCE FOR NECK BORDER

Spagnum	Blue Lovat	Foxglove	Burnt Umber
Highland Mist	Foxglove	Purple Haze	Highland Mist
Thistledown	Spagnum	Thistledown	Seaweed
Burnt Umber	Burnt Umber	Blue Lovat	Pacific
Pacific	Highland Mist	Purple Heather	Foxglove

tivoli scarf

gregory courtney

MATERIALS

YARN: Jamieson's Shetland Heather Aran (or Soft Shetland) - 100 grams each of Color A, B & C. Shown on this page in Color A, Nightshade (1401); Color B, Pine (234); and Color C, Grouse (1090). Shown on facing page in Color A, Purple Heather (239); Color B, Oceanic (692); and Color C, Gingersnap (331).
NEEDLES: US 9 (5.5 mm), *or correct needles to obtain gauge*.

MEASUREMENTS

WIDTH: 8". LENGTH (EXCLUDING FRINGE): 60".

GAUGE

On US 9 in **Brioche Stitch**: 14 sts and 20 rows = 4".

BRIOCHE STITCH (OVER EVEN NO. OF STS)

Row 1 (Foundation Row): *Yo, sl 1, k1; rep from *.
Every Row Thereafter: *Yo, sl 1, k2tog (slip st and yo of previous row); rep from *.

DESIGNER NOTES

To work a yo at the beginning of a row while joining in a color for the first time, tie the new color onto the right-hand needle before beginning the row. The strand is in place for the "k2tog" at the end of the return row. On subsequent rows, hold the yarn in front while slipping the first stitch. Don't break off colors—the next color in the sequence will always be waiting at the beginning of the appropriate row. Drop the strand just used over the new strand at the beginning of each row—this makes a tidy edge.

SCARF

With US 9 and Color A, CO 28 sts. Work in **Brioche Stitch** as follows: *1 Row Color B, 1 Row Color C, 1 Row Color A; rep from * until piece measures 60" from CO edge. With Color A, BO. *Bind off in knit using a needle 2-3 sizes larger, knitting tog the slipped st and the yo of previous row.*

ATTACH FRINGE

Cut strands of each color to desired length and attach to each end. Ours shows 1 strand of each color for each fringe.

rainbow's end vest

natalie darmohraj

MATERIALS

YARN: Jamieson's Shetland Heather Aran (or Soft Shetland) - 250 (300, 300, 350, 350, 400) grams of MC; 50 (50, 50, 50, 50, 50) grams each of Color A, B, C, D, E & F. Shown in MC, Nightshade (1401); Color A, Pippin (808); Color B, Gingersnap (331); Color C, Amethyst (1310); Color D, Husk (383); Color E, Lacquer (1220); and Color F, Oceanic (692).
NEEDLES: US 8 (5 mm), and set of double-pointed US 6 (4 mm) *or correct needles to obtain gauge.*
ACCESSORIES: Three ¾" buttons.

MEASUREMENTS

CHEST: 40 (42, 44, 46, 48, 50)".
LENGTH (EXCLUDING EDGING): 20¾ (21½, 22¼, 23, 23¾, 24½)".
LENGTH TO UNDERARM: 12½ (13, 13½, 14, 14½, 15)".
ARMHOLE DEPTH: 8¼ (8½, 8¾, 9, 9¼, 9½)".

GAUGE

On US 8 in st st: 18 sts and 24 rows = 4".

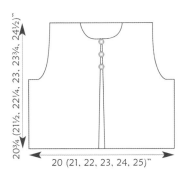

20¾ (21½, 22¼, 23, 23¾, 24½)"

20 (21, 22, 23, 24, 25)"

COLOR BLOCK SEQUENCE (WORKED OVER 12 STS ON BACK)

16 rows Color A
16 Rows Color B
16 Rows Color C
16 Rows Color D
16 Rows Color E
16 Rows Color F
16 Rows Color A

BACK

With US 8 and MC, CO 90 (96, 100, 104, 108, 114) sts. Working in st st throughout and beg with a knit row, work 6 (8, 10, 12, 14, 16) rows, ending with RS facing for next row.

BEG COLOR BLOCK SEQUENCE

Using intarsia method and continuing in st st, work 39 (42, 44, 46, 48, 51) sts in MC, work 12 (12, 12, 12, 12, 12) sts in Color A, work 39 (42, 44, 46, 48, 51) sts in MC. Continue st st and **Color Block Sequence**, **AND AT SAME TIME**, when piece measures 12½ (13, 13½, 14, 14½, 15)" from CO edge, and RS faces for next row, shape armholes as follows:

SHAPE ARMHOLES

BO 4 (4, 4, 4, 4, 4) sts at beg of next 2 rows, then 2 (2, 2, 2, 2, 2) sts at beg of following 2 rows. Dec 1 st at beg and end of next 3 rows, then on foll 3 alt rows. Continue without further shaping on rem 66 (72, 76, 80, 84, 90) sts (continuing in MC only after Color Block Sequence is complete), until armhole measures 8¼ (8½, 8¾, 9, 9¼, 9½)", ending with RS facing for next row.

SHAPE SHOULDERS

BO 6 (7, 7, 8, 8, 9) sts at beg of next 2 rows.

Next Row (RS): BO 6 (7, 7, 8, 9, 9) sts, work until there are 9 (10, 11, 11, 12, 13) sts on right-hand needle, turn.
Next Row (WS): BO 3 (3, 3, 3, 3, 3) sts, work to end of row.
Next Row (RS): BO rem 6 (7, 8, 8, 9, 10) sts.

With RS facing, rejoin yarn to rem sts, BO next 24 (24, 26, 26, 26, 28) sts for back neck, work to end of row. Shape left shoulder same as for right shoulder, **reversing shaping**.

LEFT FRONT

With MC, CO 44 (47, 49, 51, 53, 56) sts. Work in st st until piece measures 12½ (13, 13½, 14, 14½, 15)" from CO edge, ending with RS facing for next row.

SHAPE ARMHOLE

BO 4 (4, 4, 4, 4, 4) sts at beg of next row. Work 1 row. BO 2 (2, 2, 2, 2, 2) sts at beg of next row. Work 1 row. Dec 1 st at beg of next 3 rows, then following 3 alt rows. Work without further shaping on rem 32 (35, 37, 39, 41, 44) sts until piece measures 2" less than back to shoulder, ending with WS facing for next row.

SHAPE FRONT NECK

BO at neck edge 6 (6, 7, 7, 7, 8) sts once, 3 (3, 3, 3, 3, 3) sts once, 2 (2, 2, 2, 2, 2) sts once, then dec 1 st on next and following 2 alt rows. Work without further shaping on rem 18 (21, 22, 24, 26, 28) sts until armhole measures 8¼ (8½, 8¾, 9, 9¼, 9½)", ending with RS facing for next row.

SHAPE SHOULDER

Next Row (RS): BO 6 (7, 7, 8, 8, 9) sts, work to end of row.
Next Row (WS): Purl.
Next Row (RS): BO 6 (7, 7, 8, 9, 9) sts, work to end of row.
Next Row (WS): Purl.
Next Row (RS): BO rem 6 (7, 8, 8, 9, 10) sts.

RIGHT FRONT

Work same as for left front, **reversing shaping**.

FINISHING

Sew shoulder and side seams. Place a marker on center edge of right front 6 (8, 10, 12, 14, 16) rows from bottom.

CORDED EDGING

With US 6 double-pointed needle and Color C, RS facing, beg at right side seam, work corded edging as follows:

CO 3 sts, pick up 1 st at bottom edge of vest, slide sts to opposite end of needle. *k2, K2tog tbl, pick up 1 st, slide sts to opposite end of needle; rep from *, picking up 1 st in every st horizontally and 3 sts for every 4 rows vertically, continuing along bottom edge of back and along bottom edge of right front. When you reach marker, work 12 rows each in Color A, B, C, D, E and F, then Color A again, **AND AT SAME TIME**, work cord unattached to form button loops at beg of Color F and 2nd occurrence of Color A. Change to Color C, work another button loop, then continue around neck edge. Work color sequence on left front to match right front, then continue around with Color C to right side seam. BO sts and sew bound-off edge to cast-on edge of knitted cord. With Color C, work corded edging around armhole openings, beg and ending at underarm. Weave in ends. Block gently. Sew buttons opposite button loops.

marguerite beaded shawl

s a n d i   r o s n e r

MATERIALS

YARN: Jamieson's Shetland Ultra Lace - 175 grams. Shown in Natural White (104).
NEEDLES: 24" circular US 5 (3.75 mm), *or correct needle to obtain gauge*. 1 mm crochet hook.
ACCESSORIES: Approx. 1,200 4 mm round glass beads in assorted pale colors.

MEASUREMENTS (AFTER BLOCKING, NOT INCLUDING FRINGE)

WIDTH: 24".
LENGTH: 72".

GAUGE (AFTER BLOCKING)

On US 5 in **Chart**: 22 sts = 4½" and 32 rows = 4".

Key

☐	k.
—	p on right side rows; k on wrong side rows.
╱	k2tog.
╲	ssk.
O	yo.
⌒⌒⌒	sl 3 sts pwise wyif.
B	place bead and knit (see **Notes on Knitting with Beads**).

NOTES ON KNITTING WITH BEADS

Place beads individually where indicated on **Chart**. When you come to the beaded stitch, place crochet hook through one bead, remove stitch from knitting needle and use crochet hook to draw stitch through bead, then replace stich on knitting needle and knit it.

SHAWL

With US 5, CO 125 sts.

Row 1 (WS): Knit.

Next 7 Rows: Sl 3 sts pwise wyif, knit to end of row.

Work **Chart** until piece measures approx. 65" *(your shawl will gain about 7" in length after blocking)*, ending after working Row 7 of **Chart**.

Next 7 Rows: Sl 3 sts pwise wyif, knit to end of row.

FINISHING

Weave in ends. Block to finished measurements.

MAKE AND ATTACH FRINGE

Cut approximately 500 strands 10" long. Tie groups of 4 strands every other st along both ends of shawl. Tie remaining beads into fringe at random, pull strand through bead with crochet hook and secure bead with overhand knot.

Chart

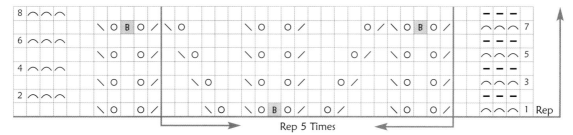

Rep 5 Times

valley of the moon vest

betsy westman

MATERIALS

YARN: Jamieson's 2-Ply Shetland Spindrift - 125 (125, 150, 150) grams of Dark Navy (730); 50 grams each of Blue Danube (134); Cloud (764); Granite (122); Green Mist (274); Mist (180); Sky (130); Surf (135); and Wild Violet (153).
NEEDLES: 16" and 24" circular US 3 (3.25 mm), *or correct needle to obtain gauge*.
ACCESSORIES: Seven ½" buttons.

MEASUREMENTS

CHEST: 37 (40, 44, 48)".
LENGTH TO ARMHOLE: 10 (10, 10, 10)".
ARMHOLE DEPTH: 10 (10, 10, 10)".
LENGTH: 20 (20, 20, 20)".

GAUGE

On US 3 in **Chart**: 28 sts and 29 rows = 4".

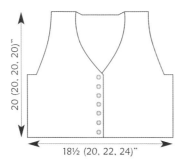

20 (20, 20, 20)"

18½ (20, 22, 24)"

NOTES ON CHART

Read odd-numbered (RS) rows from right to left and even-numbered (WS) rows from left to right. Work stars using intarsia method and strand background color throughout.

CABLED RIB PATTERN (MULTIPLE OF 4 + 2)

RT (right twist) - k1 through back loop of 2nd st, then k2tog through back loops of 1st and 2nd sts.

Row 1 (RS): *K2, p2; rep from *; end k2.
Rows 2 & 4 (WS): *P2, k2; rep from *; end p2.
Row 3 (RS): K2, p2, *RT, p2; rep from *; end k2.

Rep Rows 1-4.

BACK

With US 3 and Admiral Navy, CO 130 (138, 154, 170) sts. Work Rows 1-4 of **Cabled Rib Pattern** 4 times then work Row 1 (17 rows in all).

Next Row (WS): P65 (69, 77, 85) m1p, p65 (69, 77, 85) (131 (139, 155, 171) sts on needle).

Beg and ending at points marked for your size, work Rows 1-56 of **Chart**. BO 6 sts at beg of Row 57 and 58 as shown, then dec 1 st at beg and end of next 4 rows, then every other row 5 times, every 4th row 6 times, and every 6th row twice, as shown. Continue without further shaping on rem 85 (93, 109, 125) sts through Row 122.

SHAPE BACK NECK

On Row 123, work 24 (28, 36, 44) sts, BO 37 (37, 37, 37) sts for back neck, work 24 (28, 36, 44) sts. Turn and working each side separately, BO 4 sts at neck edge once, then dec 1 st at neck edge 5 times, as shown. BO on Row 130.

LEFT FRONT

With US 3, CO 66 (70, 78, 86) sts. Work Rows 1-4 of **Cabled Rib Pattern** 4 times then work Row 1 (17 rows in all).

Next Row (WS): Purl.

Beg and ending at points marked for your size, work portion of **Chart** for left front. Beg on Row 53, dec at neck edge every row 3 times, every other row 22 times, then every 4th row 3 times, **AND AT SAME TIME**, shape

valley of the moon vest

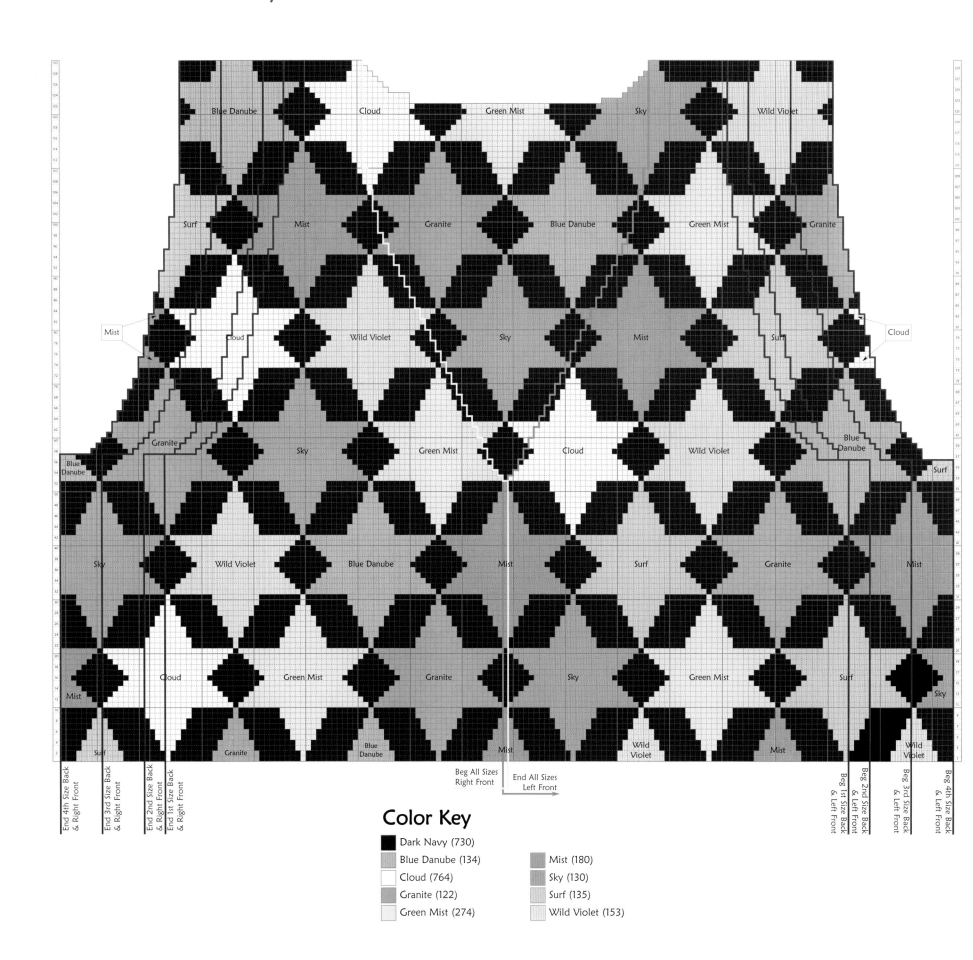

Color Key

- ■ Dark Navy (730)
- ■ Blue Danube (134)
- ■ Mist (180)
- ☐ Cloud (764)
- ■ Sky (130)
- ■ Granite (122)
- ☐ Surf (135)
- ☐ Green Mist (274)
- ☐ Wild Violet (153)

underarm as for back, as shown. Continue without further shaping and BO on Row 130.

RIGHT FRONT

With US 3, CO 66 (70, 78, 86) sts. Work Rows 1-4 of **Cabled Rib Pattern** 4 times then work Row 1 (17 rows in all).

Next Row (WS): Purl.

Beg and ending at points marked for your size, work portion of **Chart** for right front. Beg on Row 53, dec at neck edge every row 3 times, every other row 22 times, then every 4th row 3 times, **AND AT SAME TIME**, shape underarm as for back, as shown. Continue without further shaping and BO on Row 130.

FINISHING

Sew shoulders tog. Sew side seams. Weave in ends

ARMBANDS

With 16" circular US 3 and Dark Navy, RS facing, beg at underarm pick up 72 (72, 72, 72) sts up to shoulder, 1 (1, 1, 1) st in shoulder seam, and 72 (72, 72, 72) sts down to underarm (145 (145, 145, 145) sts on needle). Join, purl 1 rnd, then knit 3 rnds. BO loosely.

NECKBAND

With 24" circular US 3 and Dark Navy, RS facing, pick up 310 sts along neck edge.

Row 1 (WS): Knit.
Row 2 (RS): K4, k2tog, ([k6, k2tog] 6 times); knit to end of row.
Row 3 (WS): Purl, working a yo above k2tog's in previous row to form buttonholes.
Row 4 (RS): Knit.

BO loosely.

Sew buttons opposite buttonholes. Weave in any remaining ends. Block to finished measurements.

Karen Hall

A Visit to the Bonhoga Gallery
at the Weisdale Mill

Last summer, I had the pleasure of visiting Shetland for the second time. One of the high points of this particular trip was my visit to the Textile Museum at the Bonhoga Gallery. The gallery is situated in an historic old mill in Weisdale on the west side of Shetland. I entered through the cafe—a sunny glass atrium bordered by the mill stream. Two white-haired ladies—small in stature but certainly not in personality—sat at a table chatting as fast as they were knitting, without even looking at their work. They seemed mildly amused by my questions about their metal knitting pins and the leather belts they wore around their waists and happily answered my questions—even offering to let me try my hand at this style of knitting.

After my chat with the local ladies, I went inside to examine the textile collection. The museum itself is about the size of my yarn shop, so I felt immediately comfortable in this cozy place where everything was of interest to me. Even the postcards offered for sale—vintage images produced in postcard form—were not the usual tourist fare. Hand-knitted items were displayed in glass cases with wooden drawers below, which held smaller treasures. In one, I saw a pair of white openwork gloves, yellowed with age. They were beautiful to me because they were elegantly simple. Who in Shetland might wear gloves like these? Were they wedding gloves or were they produced for sale or trade and had missed the steamer to London or Paris? Intrigued by their simplicity, I asked the curator if she knew the pattern. She confessed she didn't and eagerly produced a large book whose bindings were well worn. The closest I could come to matching the gloves was a pattern called "Little Acre."

On the road home, with the strains of Aly Bain and his fiddle playing in the background, I began working out the pattern in my mind. The prospect of reproducing knitted gloves that were also openwork was daunting. I thought about the Shetland women in old photographs and in books I had seen. They were hard-working women, knitting during times when their hands would otherwise be idle. They would have had little use for fancy gloves. I decided to make the pattern into a wrap—something warm, practical and simple. My Bonhoga Wrap will surely not pass through a wedding ring, as Shetland lore dictates. I see in my imagination, instead, a determined Shetland woman of yesteryear wearing this wrap while carrying a burden of peat on her back, thinking of the fire at home and knitting all the way.

Karen Hall is the proprietor of Wool Gathering, a fine knitting store in Kennett Square, Pennsylvania, which specializes in quality natural fibers.

bonhoga wrap

MATERIALS
YARN: Jamieson's Shetland Heather Aran (or Soft Shetland) - 750 grams. Shown in Grouse (1090).
NEEDLES: 24" circular US 8, *or correct needles to obtain gauge*.

MEASUREMENTS (AFTER BLOCKING)
WIDTH: Approx. 30".
LENGTH: Approx. 72".

GAUGE
On US 8 in st st: 20 sts and 24 rows = 4".

DESIGNER NOTE
To calculate yardage for a shorter or longer wrap, one 50 gram skein equals approx. 5½" in length.

LACE PATTERN (MULTIPLE OF 6 + 2)
Row 1 (RS): Sl 1 pwise, k1; *yo, k2tog, ssk, yo, k2; rep from *.
Row 2 (WS): Sl 1 pwise, purl to end of row.

Rep Rows 1-2.

WRAP
With US 8, CO 140 sts. Work **Lace Pattern** until piece measures approx. 70" (or desired length). BO on Row 2 of pattern.

FINISHING
Weave in ends. Block to finished measurements. *Your wrap will gain 2" or more in both length and width, depending on how aggressively you block it.*

eliza cardigan

betsy westman

MATERIALS

YARN: Jamieson's Shetland Chunky Marl (or Chunky Shetland) - 700 (700, 800, 900) grams. Shown in Twilight (2106).
NEEDLES: 24" circular US 9 (5.5 mm) and 29" circular US 10 (6 mm), *or correct needles to obtain gauge.*
ACCESSORIES: Eight 1" buttons. Stitch markers. Stitch holders.

MEASUREMENTS

CHEST: 41 (44, 47, 50)".
LENGTH TO ARMHOLE: 18 (18, 17, 17)
ARMHOLE DEPTH: 9 (9, 10, 10)".
LENGTH: 27 (27, 27, 27)".
SLEEVE LENGTH (TO UNDERARM): 17 (17, 17, 17)".
SLEEVE LENGTH (TO SHOULDER): 22½ (22½, 22½, 22½)".

GAUGE

On US 10 in st st: 14 sts and 20 rows = 4".

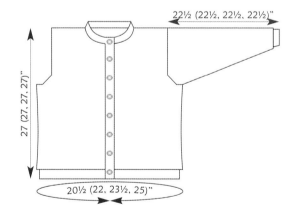

22½ (22½, 22½, 22½)"

27 (27, 27, 27)"

20½ (22, 23½, 25)"

NOTES ON CHART

Only RS rows are shown; work from right to left. Purl all WS rows.

2x2 RIB (MULTIPLE OF 4 + 2)

Row 1 (RS): K2; *p2, k2; rep from *.
Row 2 (WS): P2; *k2, p2; rep from *.

Rep Rows 1-2.

2x2 RIB FOR FRONT BANDS AND NECK BAND (MULTIPLE OF 4 + 2)

Row 1 (WS): P2; *k2, p2; rep from *.
Row 2 (RS): K2; *p2, k2; rep from *.

Rep Rows 1-2.

BODY (WORKED IN ONE PIECE TO UNDERARM)

With US 10, CO 142 (154, 162, 174) sts. Work in **2x2 Rib** for 6 rows. In last row of ribbing (WS), *inc* 1 st if working 1st or 3rd size, or *dec* 1 st if working 2nd or 4th size (143 (153, 163, 173) sts on needle). Work **Chart, AND AT SAME TIME,** on Row 34 (WS) set up markers for waist shaping as follows: p21 (21, 21, 21); place marker; p38 (42, 45, 49); place marker; p26 (28, 31, 33); place marker; p37 (41, 45, 49); place marker; p21 (21, 21, 21).

Next Row (RS): Work to 1st marker; slip marker; ssk; work to 2 sts before 2nd marker; k2tog; slip marker; work to 3rd marker; slip marker; ssk; work to 2 sts before 4th marker; k2tog; slip marker; work to end of row.

Continuing **Chart** as set, *dec* as described above after first marker, before 2nd marker, after 3rd marker and before 4th marker every 6th row 2 (2, 2, 2) more times (131 (141, 151, 161) sts on needle), then *inc* (knit into back and front of st) after first marker, before 2nd marker, after 3rd marker and before 4th marker every 8th row 3 (3, 3, 3) times (143 (153, 163, 173) sts on needle).

Continue without further shaping until piece measures 18 (18, 17, 17)" from CO edge, ending with RS facing for next row.

DIVIDE FRONTS AND BACK

Work 31 (34, 37, 39) sts (right front), BO 8 (8, 8, 10) sts, work 65 (69, 73, 75) sts (back), BO 8 (8, 8, 10) sts, k31 (34, 37, 39) sts. Place sts for right front and back on separate holders and work on left front sts only as follows:

LEFT FRONT

Beg with WS row, continuing **Chart** as set, dec 1 st at armhole edge on every row 3 (3, 3, 3) times, then every other row 2 (2, 2, 2) times. Continue without further shaping on rem 26 (29, 32, 34) sts until armhole measures 5 (5, 6, 6)", ending with WS facing for next row.

SHAPE NECK

Next Row (WS): BO 3 (3, 3, 3) sts at neck edge, work to end of row.

Continuing in st st, dec 1 st at neck edge on every row 4 (5, 6, 7) times, then every other row 2 (2, 2, 2) times. Continue without further shaping on rem 17 (19, 21, 22) sts until armhole measures 9 (9, 10, 10)". Place shoulder sts on holders.

BACK

Place back sts onto needle, rejoin yarn, and beg with WS row, continue in st st, dec'g 1 st at beg and end of every row 3 (3, 3, 3) times, then every other row 2 (2, 2, 2) times. Continue without further shaping on rem 55 (59, 63, 64) sts until armhole measures 8 (8, 9, 9)", ending with RS facing for next row.

SHAPE BACK NECK

Next Row (RS): K19 (21, 23, 24), BO 17 (17, 17, 17) sts for back neck, k19 (21, 23, 24).

Turn and working each side separately, dec 1 st at neck edge every row 2 (2, 2, 2) times (17 (19, 21, 22) sts on needle). Purl 1 WS row. Place shoulder sts on holder.

RIGHT FRONT

Place right front sts onto needle, rejoin yarn, and beg with WS row, continue **Chart** as set, dec'g 1 st at armhole edge on every row 3 (3, 3, 3) times, then every other row 2 (2, 2, 2) times. Continue without further shaping on rem 26 (29, 32, 34) sts until armhole measures 5 (5, 6, 6)", ending with RS facing for next row.

SHAPE NECK

Next Row (RS): BO 3 (3, 3, 3) sts at neck edge, work to end of row.

Continuing in st st, dec 1 st at neck edge on every row 4 (5, 6, 7) times, then every other row 2 (2, 2, 2) times. Continue without further shaping on rem 17 (19, 21, 22) sts until armhole measures 9 (9, 10, 10)". Place shoulder sts on holders.

JOIN SHOULDERS

Join shoulders using 3-needle bind-off method.

SLEEVES

With US 10, CO 34 (34, 38, 38) sts. Work **2x2 Rib** for 6 rows, inc'g 2 (2, 2, 2) sts evenly in last (WS) row (36 (36, 40, 40) sts on needle). Change to st st, **AND AT SAME TIME,** inc 1 st at beg and end of 3rd row 1 (1, 1, 1) time, then every 6th row 12 (12, 7, 7) times, then every 4th row 0 (0, 6, 6) times (62 (62, 68, 68) sts on needle). Work without further shaping until piece measures 17 (17, 17, 17)" from CO edge, ending with RS facing for next row.

SHAPE SLEEVE CAP

BO 4 (4, 4, 4) sts at beg of next 2 rows, then dec 1 st at beg and end of next 3 rows, then every other row 3 (3, 3, 3) times, every 4th row 1 (1, 1, 1) time, every other row 3 (3, 3, 3) times, then every row 7 (7, 7, 7) times (20 (20, 26, 26) sts on needle. BO.

FINISHING

Sew sleeves into armholes. Sew side and sleeve seams.

LEFT FRONT BAND

With US 9, RS facing, pick up 90 (90, 90, 90) sts along left front edge (excluding neck shaping). Work **2x2 Rib for Front Bands and Neck Band.** BO in pattern.

RIGHT FRONT BAND

With US 9, RS facing, pick up 90 (90, 90, 90) sts along right front edge (excluding neck shaping). Work **2x2 Rib for Front Bands and Neck Band, AND AT SAME TIME,** in Row 2, work buttonholes as follows: work 6 sts, p2tog, yo, ([work 10 sts, p2tog, yo] 6 times); work 10 sts.

NECK BAND

With US 9, RS facing, pick up 70 (70, 74, 74) sts evenly around neck edge, including tops of front bands. Work **2x2 RIB FOR FRONT BANDS AND NECK BAND,** for 4 rows, **AND AT SAME TIME,** in Row 2, work 1 buttonhole as follows: k2, p2tog, yo, work to end of row.

Weave in ends. Sew buttons opposite buttonholes. Block to finished measurements.

Chart

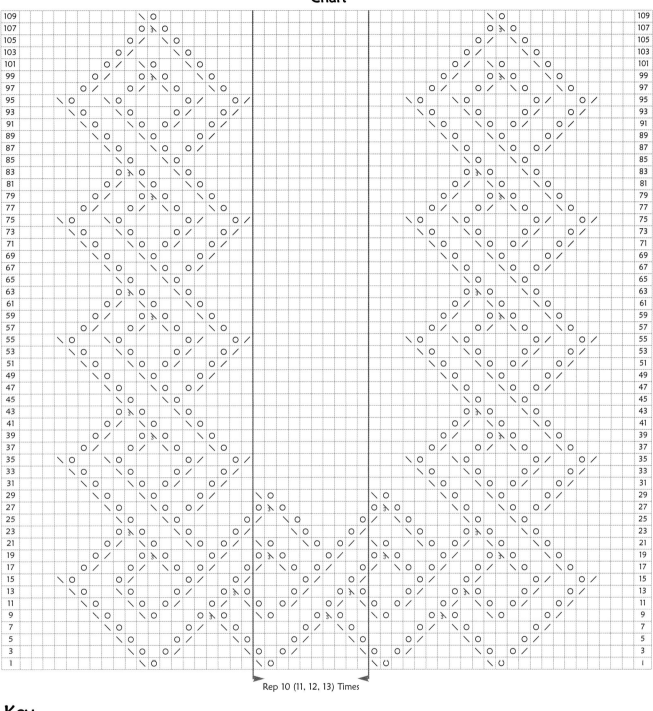

Rep 10 (11, 12, 13) Times

Key

☐	k.
╱	k2tog.
╲	ssk.
○	yo.
⅄	sl1, k2tog, psso.

hudson bay pullover

sandi rosner

MATERIALS

YARN: Jamieson's Shetland Heather Aran (or Soft Shetland) -
250 (350, 400, 450, 450) grams of MC, Ivory (343);
Jamieson's 2-Ply Shetland Spindrift - 50 (50, 50, 75, 75)
grams of Color A, Black (999); 25 (50, 50, 50, 50) grams
each of Color B, Royal (700); Color C, Cornfield (410); Color
D, Crimson (525); and Color E, Tartan (800).
NEEDLES: 16" and 24" circular US 5 (3.75 mm) and 24" circular
US 7 (4.5 mm), *or correct needles to obtain gauge*.
ACCESSORIES: Stitch holders.

MEASUREMENTS
CHEST: 32 (36, 40, 44, 48)".
LENGTH: 21 (24½, 24½, 28, 28)".
SLEEVE LENGTH: 14 (16, 18, 18, 18)".

GAUGE
On US 7 in st st: 18 sts and 24 rows = 4"

NOTES ON YARN
Work 2 strands of 2-Ply Shetland Spindrift held together
throughout. Work 1 strand of Soft Shetland throughout.

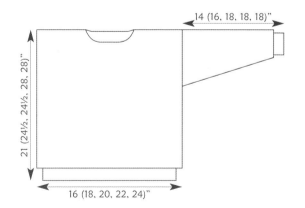

14 (16, 18, 18, 18)"

21 (24½, 24½, 28, 28)"

16 (18, 20, 22, 24)"

NOTES ON WORKING SHORT ROWS
Work stripes with short rows. To prevent a hole when
turning at end of short row, wrap stitch as follows: with
yarn to WS, slip next stitch to right-hand needle. Bring
yarn to RS and slip stitch back to left-hand needle. Turn
and knit or purl as indicated. You have wrapped working
yarn around last unworked stitch. This is abbreviated in
instructions as **W&T** for "wrap and turn." When working
back across full length of row, pick up wraps so they
won't show in the finished garment as follows: use point
of right-hand needle to lift wrap onto tip of left-hand
needle, then knit or purl wrap together with stitch. You
may need to fiddle with the wrap so it lies on WS and
doesn't show through to RS.

SLEEVE STRIPE SEQUENCE
*2 rows MC. 2 rows Color B.
2 rows MC. 2 rows Color B.
2 rows MC. 2 rows Color C.
2 rows MC. 2 rows Color C.
2 rows MC. 2 rows Color A.
2 rows MC. 2 rows Color A.
2 rows MC. 2 rows Color D.
2 rows MC. 2 rows Color D.
2 rows MC. 2 rows Color E.
2 rows MC. 2 rows Color E.
Rep from *****.

RIGHT LEANING WEDGE
With CC, knit 1 row, purl 1 row.
With MC, k60 (69, 78, 87, 96), W&T, purl back to beg.
With CC, k50 (57, 65, 72, 79), W&T, purl back to beg.
With MC, k40 (45, 52, 57, 62), W&T, purl back to beg.
With CC, k30 (33, 39, 42, 45), W&T, purl back to beg.
With MC, k20 (21, 26, 27, 28), W&T, purl back to beg.
With CC, k10 (11, 13, 12, 11), W&T, purl back to beg.
With MC, knit to end of row, picking up wraps as you
come to them. Purl 1 row. Knit 1 row.

LEFT LEANING WEDGE
With CC, purl 1 row, knit 1 row.
With MC, p60 (69, 78, 87, 96), W&T, knit back to beg.
With CC, p50 (57, 65, 72, 79), W&T, knit back to beg.
With MC, p40 (45, 52, 57, 62), W&T, knit back to beg.

With CC, p30 (33, 39, 42, 45), W&T, knit back to beg.
With MC, p20 (21, 26, 27, 28), W&T, knit back to beg.
With CC, p10 (11, 13, 12, 11), W&T, knit back to beg.
With MC, purl to end of row, picking up wraps as you come to them. Knit 1 row. Purl 1 row.

BACK
With US 5 and Color A, CO 71 (80, 89, 98, 107) sts.

Row 1 (WS): P2; *k1, p2; rep from * to end of row.
Row 2 (RS): Change to MC. K2; *p1, k2; rep from * to end of row.

Rep Rows 1 and 2 with MC until piece measures 3 (3, 3, 3, 3)" from CO edge, ending with RS facing for next row.

Change to US 7 and work 2 rows in st st.

With Color B as CC, work **Right Leaning Wedge.**
With Color C as CC, work **Left Leaning Wedge.**
With Color A as CC, work **Right Leaning Wedge.**
With Color D as CC, work **Left Leaning Wedge.**
With Color E as CC, work **Right Leaning Wedge.**
With Color B as CC, work **Left Leaning Wedge.**
With Color C as CC, work **Right Leaning Wedge.**
With Color A as CC, work **Left Leaning Wedge.**
With Color D as CC, work **Right Leaning Wedge.**
With Color E as CC, work **Left Leaning Wedge.**

For 1st size, go to **Shape Back Neck**. Continue as follows for 2nd, 3rd, 4th & 5th sizes:

With Color B as CC, work **Right Leaning Wedge.**
With Color C as CC, work **Left Leaning Wedge.**

For 2nd and 3rd sizes, go to **Shape Back Neck**. Continue as follows for 4th & 5th sizes:

With Color A as CC, work **Right Leaning Wedge.**
With Color D as CC, work **Left Leaning Wedge.**

SHAPE BACK NECK
With MC, k23 (25, 27, 32, 36) sts and place these stitches on a holder; BO next 25 (30, 35, 34, 35) sts; k23 (25, 27, 32, 36) sts and place these stitches on another holder.

FRONT
With US 5 and Color A, CO 71 (80, 89, 98, 107) sts. Work ribbing as for back.

Change to US 7 and work 2 rows in st st. Break yarn.

As you begin the Left Leaning Wedge, you will be starting with a WS row. Push the work to the opposite point of the circular needle and join yarn on the right-hand side, ready to purl the next row.

With Color B as CC, work **Left Leaning Wedge.**
With Color C as CC, work **Right Leaning Wedge.**
With Color A as CC, work **Left Leaning Wedge.**
With Color D as CC, work **Right Leaning Wedge.**
With Color E as CC, work **Left Leaning Wedge.**
With Color B as CC, work **Right Leaning Wedge.**
With Color C as CC, work **Left Leaning Wedge.**
With Color A as CC, work **Right Leaning Wedge.**

For 1st size, go to **Shape Front Neck**. Continue as follows for 2nd, 3rd, 4th & 5th sizes:

With Color D as CC, work **Left Leaning Wedge.**
With Color E as CC, work **Right Leaning Wedge.**

For 2nd and 3rd sizes, go to **Shape Front Neck**. Continue as follows for 4th and 5th sizes:

With Color B as CC, work **Left Leaning Wedge**
With Color C as CC, work **Right Leaning Wedge.**

SHAPE FRONT NECK
Continuing sequence of CC's as set, shape neck as follows:

With CC, purl 1 row, knit 1 row.
With MC, purl 1 row, knit 1 row.

Next Row (WS): With CC, p27 (29, 31, 36, 40); place rem sts on holder.
Next Row (RS): With CC, k1, ssk, knit to end of row.
Next Row (WS): With MC, purl.
Next Row (RS): With MC, k1, ssk, knit to end of row.
Next Row (WS): With CC, purl.
Next Row (RS): With CC, k1, ssk, knit to end of row.
Next Row (WS): With MC, purl.
Next Row (RS): With MC, k1, ssk, knit to end of row.
Next Row (WS): With CC, purl.
Next Row (RS): With CC, knit.
Next Row (WS): With MC, purl.
Next Row (RS): With MC, knit.
Next Row (WS): With next CC, purl.
Next Row (RS): With next CC, knit.

With MC, work 3 rows in st st. Place shoulder sts on holder.

Place stitches from holder onto needle and rejoin MC at right neck edge; BO 17 (22, 27, 26, 27) sts; purl to end of row.

Next Row (RS): With CC, knit to 3 sts from end of row, k2tog, k1.
Next Row (WS): With CC, purl.
Next Row (RS): With MC, knit to 3 sts from end of row, k2tog, k1.
Next Row (WS): With MC, purl.
Next Row (RS): With CC, knit to 3 sts from end of row, k2tog, k1.
Next Row (WS): With CC, purl.
Next Row (RS): With MC, knit to 3 sts from end of row, k2tog, k1.
Next Row (WS): With MC, purl.
Next Row (RS): With CC, knit.
Next Row (WS): With CC, purl.
Next Row (RS): With MC, knit.
Next Row (WS): With MC, purl.
Next Row (RS): With CC, knit.
Next Row (WS): With CC, purl.

With MC, work 3 rows in st st. Place shoulder sts on holder.

JOIN SHOULDERS
Join shoulders using 3-needle bind-off method.

SLEEVES
With US 5 and Color A, CO 38 (41, 44, 47, 47) sts. Work in ribbing as for back until piece measures 2 (2½, 3, 3, 3)" from CO edge.

Change to US 7 and work st st in **Sleeve Stripe Sequence**, **AND AT SAME TIME**, inc 1 st at beg and end of every 4th row 15 (20, 23, 26, 26) times (68 (81, 90, 99, 99) sts on needle). Continue without further shaping until piece measures 14 (16, 18, 18, 18)" from CO edge. BO.

FINISHING
Center sleeves at shoulder seams and sew to body. Sew side and sleeve seams.

NECKBAND
With 16" circular US 5 and MC, RS facing, pick up 25 (30, 35, 36, 35) sts along back neck edge, 12 (12, 12, 12, 12) sts down left front neck edge, 17 (21, 28, 27, 28) sts along front neck edge, and 12 (12, 12, 12, 12) sts up right front neck edge (66 (75, 87, 87, 87) sts on needle). Work in k2, p1 ribbing for 1½ (1½, 1½, 1½, 1½)". Change to Color A and work 1 row in ribbing. With Color A, BO loosely in ribbing.

Weave in ends. Block to finished measurements.

hudson bay hat

sandi rosner

MATERIALS

YARN: Jamieson's Shetland Heather Aran (or Soft Shetland) - 50 grams of MC, Ivory (343); Jamieson's 2-Ply Shetland Spindrift - 25 grams each of Color A, Black (999); Color B, Royal (700); Color C, Cornfield (410); Color D, Crimson (525); and Color E, Tartan (800).
NEEDLES: 16" circular US 5 (3.75 mm); 16" circular and set of 4 double-pointed US 7 (4.5 mm), *or correct needles to obtain gauge.*
ACCESSORIES: Stitch markers.

MEASUREMENTS

CIRCUMFERENCE: 16 (18½, 21)".

GAUGE

On US 7 in st st: 18 sts and 24 rows = 4"

YARN NOTES

Work 2 strands of 2-Ply Shetland Spindrift held together throughout. Work 1 strand of Soft Shetland throughout.

RIBBING PATTERN

Every Rnd: *P2, k1; rep from * to end of rnd.

STRIPE SEQUENCE

*2 rows MC. 2 rows Color B.
2 rows MC. 2 rows Color B.
2 rows MC. 2 rows Color C.
2 rows MC. 2 rows Color C.
2 rows MC. 2 rows Color A.
2 rows MC. 2 rows Color A.
2 rows MC. 2 rows Color D.
2 rows MC. 2 rows Color D.
2 rows MC. 2 rows Color E.
2 rows MC. 2 rows Color E.

Rep from *.

HAT

With US 5 and Color A, CO 72 (84, 96) sts. Mark beg of rnd, join, and work 1 rnd in **Ribbing Pattern**. Change to MC and continue in **Ribbing Pattern** until piece measures 2 (2, 2)" from CO edge.

Change to US 7 and work st st (knit every rnd) in **Stripe Sequence** until piece measures 8 (9, 10)" from CO edge.

SHAPE CROWN

Next Rnd: *K12 (14, 16), place marker, rep from * to end of rnd.
Next Rnd (Dec Rnd): *Knit to 2 sts before marker, k2tog, rep from * to end of rnd.

Rep **Dec Rnd**, changing to double-pointed needles when necessary, until 6 sts rem.

FINISHING

Break yarn, leaving about a 4" tail. Thread onto darning needle, draw through rem sts and push thread through hole to inside of hat. Pull tight to close hole. Weave in end.

rosemary pullover

  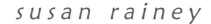

susan rainey

MATERIALS

YARN: Jamieson's Shetland Double Knitting - 475 (550, 625) grams of MC; 25 (25, 25) grams of CC. Shown in MC, Spagnum (233) and CC, Purple Heather (239).
NEEDLES: US 5 (3.75 mm), US 9 (5.5 mm) and US 7 (4.5 mm) (*US 7 is used for BO only*), **or correct needles to obtain gauge**.
ACCESSORIES: Stitch holders.

MEASUREMENTS

CHEST: 41 (45½, 50)".
LENGTH: 25 (26, 27)".
SLEEVE LENGTH (MEASURED FROM TOP OF SHOULDER TO CUFF FOLD LINE): 20 (21, 22)".

GAUGE

On US 9 in **Knit-Through Honeycomb Stitch**: 22 sts and 27 rows = 4".
On US 5 in **Shale Lace Pattern**: 25 sts and 34 rows = 4".

SPECIAL ABBREVIATIONS

K4tog - K4 sts together (3 sts decreased).
K3tog - K3 sts together (2 sts decreased).
ssssk - sl 4 sts (one at a time) kwise; knit these 4 sts together through front of sts (3 sts decreased).
sssk - sl 3 sts (one at a time) kwise; knit these 3 sts together through front of sts (2 sts decreased).

SHALE LACE PATTERN (MULTIPLE OF 14 + 1)

Row 1 (RS): P1; *k13, p1; rep from *.
Rows 2 & 4 (WS): K1; *p13, k1; rep from *.
Row 3 (RS): P1; *k4tog, ([yo, k1] 5 times), yo, ssssk, p1; rep from *.

Rep Rows 1-4

KNIT-THROUGH HONEYCOMB STITCH (MULTIPLE OF 2)

KTH (over 2 sts): Insert right-hand needle into first st as if to purl and knit second st, pulling it through first st; knit first st tbl.

Note: *Rows 1 and 3 have a slightly tighter gauge than Rows 2 and 4.*

Row 1 (RS): *KTH; rep from *.
Row 2 & 4 (WS): Purl.
Row 3 (RS): *K1, KTH; rep from * to last st; k1.

Rep Rows 1-4.

BACK

With US 5 and CC, CO 127 (141, 155) sts.

Next Row (RS): Purl.
Next Row (WS): Change to MC and purl.

Work **Shale Lace Pattern** until piece measures 4 (4½, 4½)" from longest point of scalloped bottom edge, ending after working Row 4 of pattern.

Next Row (RS): Knit, dec'g 13 (15, 17) sts evenly spaced across row (114 (126, 138) sts on needle).

Next Row (WS): Knit.

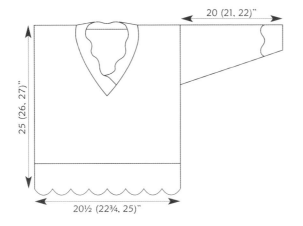

20 (21, 22)"

25 (26, 27)"

20½ (22¾, 25)"

Next Row (RS): Purl.
Next Row (WS): Change to US 9 and purl.

Work **Knit-Through Honeycomb Pattern** until piece measures 22 (23, 24)" from longest point of scalloped bottom edge, ending with RS facing for next row.

SHAPE BACK NECK

Next Row (RS): Work 46 (50, 56) sts, BO 22 (26, 26) sts for back neck, work to end of row.

Turn, and working each side separately, BO 5 sts at neck edge 1 (1, 1) time, 4 sts 0 (0, 1) time, 3 sts 2 (2, 1) time(s), 2 sts 1 (1, 2) time(s), and 1 st 5 (5, 4) times. Work without further shaping on rem 28 (32, 36) sts until piece measures 25 (26, 27)" from longest point of scalloped bottom edge. Place shoulder sts on holders.

FRONT

Work same as for back until piece measures 12 (12½, 12¾)" from longest point of scalloped bottom edge, ending with RS facing for next row.

SHAPE FRONT NECK

Next Row (RS): Work 57 (63, 69) sts and place on holder; work rem 57 (63 69) sts.

Turn, and working right front only, dec 1 st at neck edge every row 12 (14, 16) times, then every other row 10 (9, 9) times, then every 4th row 7 (8, 8) times. Work without further shaping on rem 28 (32, 36) sts until piece measures same as back. Place shoulder sts on holders. Rep for left front.

JOIN SHOULDERS

Join shoulders using 3-needle BO method.

SLEEVES

With US 5 and CC, CO 59 (67, 73) sts.

Next Row (RS): Purl.
Next Row (WS): Change to MC and purl.

SHAPE CUFF

Work **Shale Lace Pattern**, beg with Row 3 of pattern as follows, and dec'g to shape cuff as specified, for your size:

1ST AND 3RD SIZES ONLY

Next Row (RS) (Row 3 of Shale Lace Pattern) (Dec #1): P2tog; *k4tog, ([yo, k1] 5 times), yo, ssssk, p1; rep from * to last 15 sts; k4tog, ([yo, k1] 5 times), yo, ssssk, p2tog (57 (71) sts on needle).

Continue **Shale Lace Pattern** from Row 4, **AND AT SAME TIME**, dec one st near beg and end of every occurrence of Row 3 of pattern as follows:

Note: *On occurrences of Rows 1, 2 & 4 of **Shale Lace Pattern**, knit the knit sts as they face you and purl the purl sts and yo's as they face you.*

Row 3 (RS) (Dec #2): P1, k4tog, k1 ([yo, k1] 4 times), yo, ssssk, p1; *k4tog, ([yo, k1] 5 times), yo, ssssk, p1; rep from * to last 14 sts; k4tog ([yo, k1] 5 times), ssssk, p1 (55 (69) sts on needle).

Row 3 (RS) (Dec #3): P1, k4tog, ([yo, k1] 4 times), yo ssssk, p1; *k4tog, ([yo, k1] 5 times), yo, ssssk, p1; rep from * to last 13 sts; k4tog, ([yo, k1] 4 times), yo, ssssk, p1 (53 (67) sts on needle).

Row 3 (RS) (Dec #4): P1, k3tog, k1 ([yo, k1] 3 times), yo, ssssk, p1, *k4tog, ([yo, k1] 5 times), yo, ssssk, p1; rep from * to last 12 sts; k4tog, ([yo, k1] 4 times), sssk, p1 (51 (65) sts on needle).

Row 3 (RS) (Dec #5): P1, k3tog, ([yo, k1] 3 times), yo, ssssk, p1, *k4tog, ([yo, k1] 5 times), yo, ssssk, p1; rep from * to last 11 sts; k4tog, ([yo, k1] 3 times), yo, sssk, p1 (49 (63) sts on needle).

Next Row (WS): Work Row 4 of pattern.

Skip down to "**ALL SIZES.**"

2ND SIZE ONLY

Next Row (RS) (Row 3 of Shale Lace Pattern) (Dec #1): P1, k3tog, k1 ([yo, k1] 3 times), yo, ssssk, p1, *k4tog, ([yo, k1] 5 times), yo, ssssk, p1; rep from * to last 12 sts; k4tog ([yo, k1] 4 times), sssk, p1 (65 sts on needle).

Continue **Shale Lace Pattern** from Row 4, **AND AT SAME TIME**, dec one st near beg and end of every occurrence of Row 3 of pattern as follows:

Note: *On occurrences of Rows 1, 2 & 4 of **Shale Lace Pattern**, knit the knit sts as they face you and purl the purl sts and yo's as they face you.*

Row 3 (RS) (Dec #2): P1, k3tog, ([yo, k1] 3 times), yo, ssssk, p1, *k4tog, ([yo, k1] 5 times), yo, ssssk, p1; rep from * to last 11 sts; k4tog, ([yo, k1] 3 times), yo, sssk, p1 (63 sts on needle).

Row 3 (RS) (Dec #3): P1, k2tog, k1, ([yo, k1] 2 times), yo, ssssk, p1, *k4tog, ([yo, k1] 5 times), yo, ssssk, p1; rep from * to last 10 sts; k4tog ([yo, k1] 3 times), ssk, p1 (61 sts on needle).

Row 3 (RS) (Dec #4): P1, k2tog, ([yo, k1] 2 times), yo, ssssk, p1, *k4tog, ([yo, k1] 5 times), yo, ssssk, p1; rep from * to last 9 sts; k4tog ([yo, k1] 2 times), yo, ssk, p1 (59 sts on needle).

Row 3 (RS) (Dec #5): P1, k2, yo, k1, yo, ssssk, p1; *k4tog, ([yo, k1] 5 times), yo, ssssk, p1; rep from * to last 8 sts; k4tog, yo, k1, yo, k2, p1 (57 sts on needle).

Next Row (WS): Work Row 4 of pattern.

ALL SIZES
Next Row (RS): Knit, dec'g 5 (7, 7) sts evenly spaced across row (44 (50, 56) sts on needle).
Next Row (WS): Knit
Next Row (RS): Purl.
Next Row (WS): Knit.
Next Row (WS of Sleeve): Change to US 9 and purl.

Note: *Here you've reversed the RS and WS so the cuff can be turned back.*

Work **Knit-Through Honeycomb Pattern, AND AT SAME TIME,** inc 1 st at beg and end of every occurrence of Row 3 of pattern 30 (30, 30) times (104 (110, 116) sts on needle). Work without further shaping until sleeve measures 20 (21, 22)" (measured with cuff turned back at turning row). With US 7, BO.

NECKBAND
With US 5 and CC, CO 169 (183, 197) sts.

Next Row (RS): Purl.
Next Row (WS): Change to MC and purl.

Work **Shale Lace Pattern** until piece measures 2¼ (2½, 2½)" from longest point of scalloped edge, ending with WS facing for next row.

Next Row (WS): Knit.
Next Row (RS): Purl.
Next Row (WS): Purl.
Next Row (RS): With US 7, loosely BO first 56 (61, 65) sts; change to US 9 and loosely BO next 57 (61, 67) sts; change to US 7 and loosely BO rem 56 (61, 65) sts.

FINISHING
Block pieces to finished measurements, correcting slight bias which may have occurred during knitting.

ESTABLISH AND EDGE SIDE VENTS
With US 5 and MC, RS facing, pick up 24 (27, 27) sts along left side of front, between bottom edge and 2 rows of reverse stockinette stitch at top of lace pattern.

Next Row (WS): BO in knit.

Rep for right side of front, and both sides of back. *These side vents are left open when sewing up side seams.*

Center sleeves at shoulder seams and sew to body. Sew sleeve seams, reversing seam 1" above cuff fold line. Turn cuff back. Sew side seams, omitting side vents.

ATTACH COLLAR
Block collar to match neck opening. Center neckband in neck opening and sew into place, along channel formed by the purl row worked before BO. Sew short sides to front edges, overlapping right front edge over left front edge and stitching into place.

Weave in ends. Lightly steam seams. Turn cuffs back at turning row. Block to finished measurements.

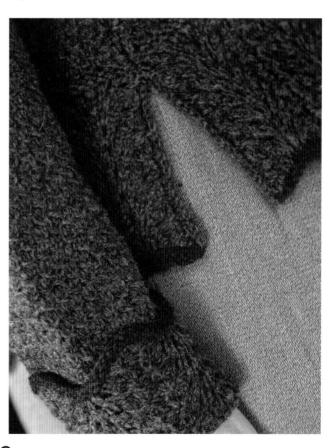

ann curly jacket

betsy westman

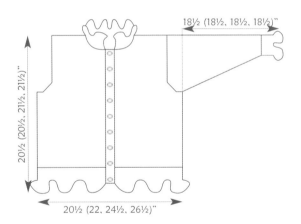

18½ (18½, 18½, 18½)"

20½ (20½, 21½, 21½)"

20½ (22, 24½, 26½)"

NOTES ON CHART

Read odd-numbered (RS) rows from right to left and even-numbered (WS) rows from left to right. To reduce the number of ends to weave in and stabilize the fabric, carry Color B across rows and along edges between rows.

SMOCKING PATTERN (MULTIPLE OF 8 + 2)

DTL (draw through loop): Insert right-hand needle between 6th and 7th sts, wrap yarn around needle and draw through a loop, slip loop to left-hand needle and ktog with 1st st on left-hand needle.

Foundation Row (RS): P2; *k2, p2; rep from *.
Rows 1, 3, 5 & 7 (WS): K2; *p2, k2; rep from *.
Row 2 & 6 (RS): P2; *k2, p2; rep from *.
Row 4 (RS): P2; *DTL, k1, p2, k2, p2; rep from *.
Row 8 (RS): P2, k2, p2; *DTL, k1, p2, k2, p2; rep from * to last 4 sts; end k2, p2.

Rep Rows 1-8.

BACK

With US 6 and Color A, CO 228 (260, 292, 340) sts. Work 6 rows in st st, ending with RS facing for next row.

Next Row (RS): *K2tog; rep from * (114 (130, 146, 170) sts rem on needle).
Next Row (WS): Purl.

Work Foundation Row of **Smocking Pattern,** Rows 1-8 twice, and Rows 1-2.

Next Row (WS): Knit, dec'g 12 (20, 24, 38) sts evenly spaced across row (102 (110, 122, 132) sts on needle.
Next Row (RS): Purl.
Next Row (WS): Purl.

Beg and ending at points marked for your size, work **Chart** until piece measures 11½ (11½, 11½, 11½)" from CO edge, ending with RS facing for next row.

SHAPE ARMHOLES

BO 4 (4, 5, 5) sts at beg of next 2 rows, then dec 1 st at beg and end of next 5 (5, 5, 5) rows, then every other row 2 (2, 3, 3) times. Work without further shaping on rem 80 (88, 96, 106) sts until armhole measures 8½ (8½, 9½, 9½)", ending with RS facing for next row.

SHAPE BACK NECK
NEXT ROW (RS): Work 22 (26, 30, 35) sts, BO 36 (36, 36, 36) sts for back neck, work 22 (26, 30, 35) sts.

Turn and working each side separately, BO 1 (1, 1, 1) st at neck edge on next 2 rows. BO rem 20 (24, 28, 33) sts.

LEFT FRONT
With US 6 and Color A, CO 116 (132, 148, 164) sts. Work 6 rows in st st, ending with RS facing for next row.

Next Row (RS): *K2tog; rep from * (58 (66, 74, 82) sts rem on needle).
Next Row (WS): Purl.

Work Foundation Row of **Smocking Pattern**, Rows 1-8 twice, and Rows 1-2.

Next Row (WS): Knit, dec'g 8 (12, 14, 16) sts evenly spaced across row (50 (54, 60, 66) sts on needle).
Next Row (RS): Purl.
Next Row (WS): Purl.

Beg and ending at points marked for your size, work **Chart** until piece measures 11½ (11½, 11½, 11½)" from CO edge, ending with RS facing for next row.

SHAPE ARMHOLE
BO 4 (4, 5, 5) sts at beg of next row, then dec 1 st at beg of next 5 (5, 5, 5) rows, then every other row 2 (2, 3, 3) times. Work without further shaping on rem 39 (43, 47, 53) sts until armhole measures 6 (6, 7, 7)", ending with WS facing for next row.

SHAPE FRONT NECK
BO 7 (7, 8, 8) sts at beg of next row, then dec 1 st at neck edge on next row; BO 3 (3, 3, 3) sts at beg of next row; dec 1 st at neck edge every row 5 (5, 5, 5) times, then every other row 3 (3, 2, 3) times. Work without further shaping on rem 20 (24, 28, 33) sts until piece measures same length as back. BO.

RIGHT FRONT
Work same as for left front, ***reversing shaping***.

SLEEVE
With US 6 and Color A, CO 100 (100, 112, 112) sts. Work 4 rows in st st, ending with RS facing for next row.

Next Row (RS): *K2tog; rep from * (50 (50, 56, 56) sts rem on needle).
Next Row (WS): Purl.

Work Foundation Row of **Smocking Pattern**, Rows 3-8, Rows 1-8, and Rows 1-2.

Next Row (WS): Knit, dec'g 10 (10, 10, 10) sts evenly spaced across row (40 (40, 46, 46) sts on needle).
Next Row (RS): Purl.
Next Row (WS): Purl, inc'g 1 st at beg and end of row (42 (42, 48, 48) sts on needle).

Beg and ending at points marked for your size work **Chart**, **AND AT SAME TIME**, inc 1 st at beg and end of every other row 2 (2, 4, 4) times, every 4th row 13 (13, 20, 20) times, and every 6th row 4 (4, 0, 0) times (80 (80, 96, 96) sts on needle). Work without further shaping until piece measures

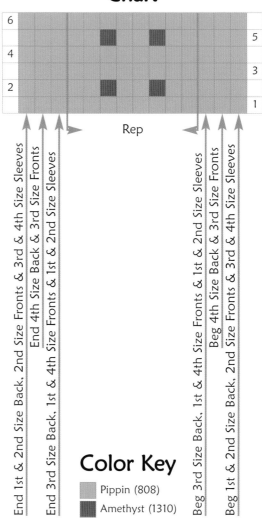

Chart

Rep

End 1st & 2nd Size Back, 2nd Size Fronts & 3rd & 4th Size Sleeves
End 4th Size Back & 3rd Size Fronts
End 3rd Size Back, 1st & 4th Size Fronts & 1st & 2nd Size Sleeves
Beg 3rd Size Back, 1st & 4th Size Fronts & 1st & 2nd Size Sleeves
Beg 4th Size Back & 3rd Size Fronts
Beg 1st & 2nd Size Back, 2nd Size Fronts & 3rd & 4th Size Sleeves

Color Key
Pippin (808)
Amethyst (1310)

18½ (18½, 18½, 18½)" from CO edge, ending with RS facing for next row.

SHAPE SLEEVE CAP

BO 4 (4, 5, 5) sts at beg of next 2 rows, then dec 1 st at beg and end of every row 6 (6, 7, 7) times, every other row 5 (5, 5, 5) times, and every row 9 (9, 10, 10) times. BO rem 32 (32, 42, 42) sts.

FINISHING

Sew shoulders tog. Center sleeves at shoulder seams and sew to body. Sew side and sleeve seams.

BUTTON BAND

With US 6 and Color A, RS facing, pick up 74 (74, 78, 78) sts evenly along right front, omitting approx. 1½" at bottom.

Row 1 & 3 (WS): P2; *k2, p2; rep from *.
Row 2 & 4 (RS): K2; *p2, k2; rep from *.

BO loosely.

BUTTONHOLE BAND

With US 6 and Color A, RS facing, pick up 74 (74, 78, 78) sts evenly along left front, omitting approx. 1½" at bottom.

Row 1 (WS) (All Sizes): P2; *k2, p2; rep from *.
Row 2 (RS) (1st & 2nd Sizes): K2; ([p1, k2tog, k1, p2, k2] 9 times).
Row 2 (RS) (3rd & 4th Sizes): K2, p2; ([k1, k2tog, p1, k2, p2] 9 times); end k2.
Row 3 (WS) (1st & 2nd Sizes): ([P2, k2, p1, yo, k2] 9 times); end p2.
Row 3 (WS) (3rd & 4th Sizes): P2; ([k2, p2, k1, yo, p2] 9 times); end k2, p2.
Row 4 (RS) (All Sizes): K2; *p2, k2; rep from *.

BO loosely.

COLLAR

With US 6 and Color A, WS facing, pick up 106 (106, 106, 106) sts evenly along neck edge, omitting buttonbands.

NOTE

The WS of jacket becomes the RS of collar; although you pick up with the WS of jacket facing, it is actually the RS of collar.

Work Rows 1-8 of **Smocking Pattern** twice, then work Rows 1-3.

Next Row (RS): *K1tbl, k1 in same st; rep from * (212 (212, 212, 212) sts on needle).

Work 5 rows in st st, beg with purl row. BO tightly.

Weave in ends. Block to finished measurements. Sew buttons opposite buttonholes.

The first time I encountered Nicky Epstein was at a knitting trade show. She approached our booth laden with knitted fruit and vegetables, a beaded lampshade and a sheep's head emerging from a pillow—a knitting shepherd seeking homes for her flock of projects. To say I was taken aback would be an understatement, yet I soon came to appreciate Nicky as one of knitting's most innovative designers. The zany projects were from her then new book, **Knitting for the Home**, which would become a top seller.

Nicky's anthology is varied and amazing—she is a master of scale and form. **Knitted Embellishments** has become a source book for knitters seeking clever closures and never-before-thought-of embellishments. She has delighted knitters and collectors alike with **Knits for Barbie™**, **Crochet for Barbie™**, and **Barbie™ Doll and Me**.

Nicky's latest books, **Knitting On the Edge** and **Knitting Over the Edge** further demonstrate her talent for seeing beyond the ordinary. Already described as essentials in any knitting library, they will challenge and inspire knitters for years to come.

Nicky continues to push the boundaries of knitting each season, appearing in national knitting magazines on a regular basis. Last year, she explored felting Shetland wool with the beautiful **Jacobean Bag** featured in **Interweave Knits**. We're glad the yarn and process were to Nicky's liking as she now presents you with Autumn Leaves Felted Bag—a whimsical shoulder bag felted in our new Shetland Heather.

autumn leaves felted bag

nicky epstein

MATERIALS

YARN: Jamieson's Shetland Heather Aran (or Soft Shetland) - 250 grams of MC, Autumn (998); 50 grams each of Pippin (808); Gingersnap (331); and Husk (383).
NEEDLES: US 10 (6 mm) and set of double-pointed US 9 (5.5 mm), *or correct needles to obtain gauge*.

MEASUREMENTS

BEFORE FELTING: 16" x 17". **APPROXIMATE SIZE AFTER FELTING*:** 14" x 11".

*Felting is not an exact science.
Your bag may be larger or smaller after it is felted.

GAUGE

On US 10 in st st: 14 sts and 18 rows = 4".

LEAVES

Make leaves in the following 2-color combinations and solid colors:

2-COLOR COMBINATIONS

Color A, Pippin/Color B, Gingersnap—make 11.
Color A, Gingersnap/Color B, Pippin—make 11.
Color A, Husk/Color B, Pippin—make 4.
Color A, Pippin/Color B, Husk—make 4.

SOLID COLORS

Color A only, Pippin—make 4.
Color A only, Gingersnap—make 4.

You'll make 18 leaves for each side of bag and 1 leaf for each handle (38 in all).

LEAF

With MC and double-pointed US 9, CO 3 sts and work cord for approx. 3" as follows: *k3; without turning work, slide sts to right-hand side of needle; rep from *.

When working solid-color leaves, work all rows with Color A only.

Row 1 (RS): With leaf color A, knit into front and back of 1st st, yo, k1, yo, knit into front and back of last st (7 sts on needle).
Row 2 (WS): With A, purl.
Row 3 (RS): With A, k3, yo, k1, yo; join B and k3 (9 sts on needle).
Row 4 (WS): With B, p4; with A, p5.
Row 5 (RS): With A, k4, yo, k1, yo; with B, k4 (11 sts on needle).
Row 6 (WS): With B, p5; with A, p6.
Row 7 (RS): With A, BO 3 sts ([k1, yo] twice); with B, k5 (10 sts on needle).
Row 8 (WS): With B, BO 3 sts, p1; with A, p5 (7 sts on needle).
Row 9 (RS): With A, k3, ([yo, k1] twice); with B, k2 (9 sts on needle).
Row 10 (WS): With B, p3; with A, p6.
Row 11 (RS): With A, k4, ([yo, k1] twice); with B, k3 (11 sts on needle).
Row 12 (WS): With B, p4; with A, p7.
Row 13 (RS): With A, BO 3 sts, ([k1, yo] twice), k1; with B, k4 (10 sts on needle).
Row 14 (WS): With B, BO 3 sts, p1; with A, p5 (7 sts on needle).
Row 15 (RS): With A, ssk, k2; with B, k1, k2tog (5 sts on needle).
Row 16 (WS): With B, p3; with A, p2.

Row 17 (RS): With A, ssk; with B, k1, k2tog (3 sts on needle).
Row 18 (WS): With B, p3.
Row 19 (RS): Sl 1, k2tog, psso. Fasten off rem st.

BAG BODY (MAKE 2)

With US 10 and MC, CO 31 sts. Knit 1 row. Continue in st st, **AND AT SAME TIME**, CO 4 sts at beg of next 8 rows, then CO 2 sts at beg of next 2 rows (67 sts on needle). Continue in st st until piece measures 3" from CO edge, ending with RS facing for next row.

SECTION 1 - ATTACH 5 LEAVES

With spare needle, pick up 3 cast-on sts of cord from WS of 1 leaf. K4 bag sts; *hold needle with 3 cord sts in front of needle with bag sts, RS facing, and using third needle, knit next 3 bag sts tog with 3 cord sts, k11 bag sts; rep from * until 5 leaves are attached; end k4 bag sts.

Work in st st for 3", ending with RS facing for next row.

SECTION 2 - ATTACH 4 LEAVES

With spare needle, pick up 3 cast-on sts of cord from WS of 1 leaf. *K11 bag sts; hold needle with 3 cord sts in front of needle with bag sts, RS facing, and using third needle, knit next 3 bag sts tog with 3 cord sts; rep from * until 4 leaves are attached.

Work in st st for 3", ending with RS facing for next row.

Rep Section 1 and Section 2 above with 3" st st between. Work in st st for 5½", ending with WS facing for next row. Purl 2 rows for turning ridge. Continue in st st for 1". BO.

POCKET

With US 10 and Husk, CO 25 sts. Work in st st for 8". BO.

HANDLE (MAKE 2)

With US 8 double-pointed needle, CO 15 sts. Work in st st for 62". BO. Sew 1 leaf onto each handle near middle.

FINISHING

Sew pocket to inside of bag. Sew 2 halves of bag together, leaving 1" unsewn at top. Fold top of bag at turning ridge and sew down, leaving openings at each end. Hook a safety pin onto a nylon stocking and pull through hem to keep from felting closed. Machine wash bag and handle with an old pair of jeans in hot/cold cycle until bag is felted. Remove from washing machine and lay flat to dry. While bag is still damp, shape any pieces that may have become distorted during washing. When bag is completely dry, push handle through hem and sew ends of handle together.

maude vest

carol lapin

MATERIALS
YARN: Jamieson's Shetland Double Knitting - 175 grams each of Color A and Color B. Shown in Color A, Port Wine (293) and Color B, Maroon (595).
NEEDLES: 32" circular US 6 (4 mm), *or correct needle to obtain gauge.*

MEASUREMENTS
WIDTH: 48". **LENGTH:** 28".

GAUGE
On US 6 in st st: 21 sts and 29 rows = 4".

DESIGNER NOTE
Work garment from side-to-side in one piece.

STRIPE SEQUENCE
Row 1 (RS): With Color B, knit.
Row 2 (WS): With Color B, purl.
Row 3 (RS): With Color A, knit.
Row 4 (WS): With Color A, purl.

Rep Rows 1-4.

VEST
With US 6 and Color A, CO 148 sts. Work in **Stripe Sequence** until piece measures 17" from CO edge, ending after working Row 2 (Color B) of **Stripe Sequence**.

MAKE ARMHOLE
Next Row (RS): With Color A, k66, BO 60 sts, k22.
Next Row (WS): With Color A, p22, CO 60 sts, p66.

Continue in **Stripe Sequence** until piece measures 14" from armhole, then **Make Armhole** again after working Row 2 (Color B) of **Stripe Sequence**. Continue in **Stripe Sequence** for another 17", ending after working Row 2 of **Stripe Sequence**. With Color A, BO in knit

FINISHING
Weave in ends. Block to finished measurements.

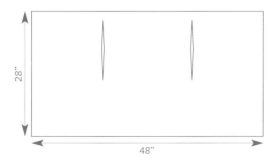

aubrey jacket

natalie darmohraj

MATERIALS
YARN: Jamieson's Shetland Heather Aran (or Soft Shetland) - 600 (650, 700) grams. Shown in Loden (848).
NEEDLES: US 7 (4.5 mm), *or correct needles to obtain gauge.*
ACCESSORIES: Four ¾" buttons.

MEASUREMENTS
CHEST: 42 (46, 50)".
LENGTH: 21 (22, 23)".
LENGTH TO UNDERARM: 12 (12½, 13)".
ARMHOLE DEPTH: 9 (9½, 10)".
SLEEVE LENGTH TO UNDERARM: 16 (16½, 17)".

GAUGE
On US 7 in **Seed Stitch**: 17 sts and 34 rows = 4".

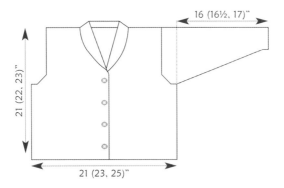

16 (16½, 17)"

21 (22, 23)"

21 (23, 25)"

SEED STITCH (ODD NO OF STITCHES)
Row 1 (RS): K1, *p1, k1; rep from *.
Row 2 (WS): Knit the purl sts and purl the knit sts as they face you.

Rep Rows 1-2.

BACK
With US 7, CO 91 (99, 107) sts. Work in **Seed Stitch** until piece measures 12 (12½, 13)" from CO edge, ending with RS facing for next row.

SHAPE ARMHOLES
BO 5 (5, 5) sts and beg of next 2 rows (81 (89, 97) sts on needle). Dec 1 st at beg and end of next and following 4 alt rows. Work without further shaping on rem (71 (79, 87) sts until armhole measures 9 (9½, 10)", ending with RS facing for next row.

SHAPE SHOULDERS AND BACK NECK
BO 7 (8, 9) sts at beg of next 2 rows.

Next Row (RS): BO 7 (8, 9) sts, work until there are 10 (11, 12) sts on right-hand needle, turn.
Next Row (WS): BO 4 (4, 4) sts; work to end of row.
Next Row (RS): BO rem 6 (7, 8) sts.

With RS facing, rejoin yarn to rem sts, BO next 23 (25, 27) sts for back neck, work to end of row.

Shape left shoulder same as for right shoulder, *reversing shaping.*

LEFT FRONT
With US 7, CO 51 (55, 59) sts. Work in **Seed Stitch** until piece measures 12 (12½, 13)" from CO edge, ending with RS facing for next row.

SHAPE ARMHOLE
BO 5 (5, 5) sts at beg of next row (46 (50, 54) sts on needle). Work 1 row. Dec 1 st at beg of next and following 4 alt rows (41 (45, 49) sts on needle). Work 1 row.

BEGIN COLLAR AND SHAPE FRONT NECK
Next Row (RS) (Collar Inc Row): Work to last st, m1, k1.

Continue as set, working **Collar Inc Row** every 6th row 9 more times (51 (55, 59) sts on needle). **AT SAME TIME,** when armhole measures 9 (9½, 10)", and RS faces for next row, shape shoulder as follows:

SHAPE SHOULDERS AND COMPLETE COLLAR
BO 7 (8, 9) sts at beg of next 2 RS rows. BO 6 (7, 8) sts at beg of next RS row. Continue on rem 31 (32, 33) collar sts until collar fits comfortably along back neck edge to center of back neck. BO collar sts.

Mark position for 4 buttons along front edge—the 1st button 1" below beg of collar shaping, the 4th button 1½" from bottom edge and the 2nd and 3rd buttons spaced evenly between the 1st and 4th.

RIGHT FRONT

Work same as for left front, *reversing shaping*, **AND AT SAME TIME**, make 4 button-holes to correspond with button markers as follows:

Buttonhole Row (RS): K1, p1, k1, k2tog, yo, work to end of row.

SLEEVES

With US 7, CO 41 (43, 45) sts. Work in **Seed Stitch, AND AT SAME TIME**, inc 1 st at beg and end of 7th row once, then every following 6th row 8 (9, 10) times, then every 8th row 9 (9, 9) times (77 (81, 85) sts on needle). Continue without further shaping until sleeve measures 16 (16½, 17)" from CO edge, ending with RS facing for next row.

SHAPE SLEEVE CAP

BO 5 (5, 5) sts at beg of next 2 rows, then dec 1 st at beg and end of next row and following 4 alternate rows. Work 1 row. BO.

FINISHING

Sew shoulder seams. Sew collar along back neck edge. Sew bound-off ends of collar tog at center of back neck. Center sleeves at shoulder seams and sew to body. Sew side and sleeve seams. Sew buttons opposite buttonholes. Weave in ends. Block to finished measurements.

aubrey cap

s u s a n   r a i n e y

NOTES ON CHART
Read odd-numbered (RS) rows from right to left and even-numbered (WS) rows from left to right.

MAIN BODY
With US 7, CO 20 sts.

Next Row (WS): K1, p1, k1, p1, m1p, p2, k1, p2, m1p, p2, m1p, p2, k1, p2, m1p, p1, k1, p1, k1 (24 sts on needle).

Work **Chart** until piece measures 21" from CO edge, ending with RS facing for next row.

Next Row (RS): P1, k1 into st below, p1, k1, k2tog, k1, p1 ([k1, k2tog] twice), k2, p1, k1, k2tog, k1, p1, k1 into st below, p1 (20 sts rem).

BO. Sew CO and BO edges tog to form back seam.

BRIM
With circular US 6, beg at back seam, pick up 108 sts evenly spaced around bottom edge of main body, place marker, join, and work 6 rnds as follows: ⸲k2, p2; rep from ⸲. BO in pattern.

TOP
With circular US 6, beg at back seam, pick up 112 sts evenly spaced around top edge of main body, place marker, join, and work in st st in the rnd until hat measures 5" (measured from bottom of brim). *You'll only knit a few rnds before you begin shaping the crown.*

SHAPE CROWN
When sts become too stretched, change to double-pointed needles.

Rnd 1 (Dec Rnd 1): ([K6, k2tog] 14 times) (98 sts rem).
Rnd 2, 3, 4, 6, 7, 8, 10, 11, 13, 14, 16 & 18: Knit.
Rnd 5 (Dec Rnd 2): ([K5, k2tog] 14 times) (84 sts rem).
Rnd 9 (Dec Rnd 3): ([K4, k2tog] 14 times) (70 sts rem).
Rnd 12 (Dec Rnd 4): ([K3, k2tog] 14 times) (56 sts rem).
Rnd 15 (Dec Rnd 5): ([K2, k2tog] 14 times) (42 sts rem).
Rnd 17 (Dec Rnd 6): ([K1, k2tog] 14 times) (28 sts rem).
Rnd 19 (Dec Rnd 7): ([K2tog] 7 times) (14 sts rem).
Rnd 20 (Dec Rnd 8): ([K2tog] 7 times) (7 sts rem).
Rnd 21 (Dec Rnd 9): ([K2tog] twice), k3tog. Leave rem 3 sts on needle.

MAKE TOP KNOT
With two US 6 double-pointed needles, work as follows:

Every Row: K3; without turning, slide sts to other end of needle, pull yarn tightly across back.

Rep this row until cord measures 3". Break yarn, leaving 8" tail. Thread onto darning needle and draw through rem sts. Tie cord into a knot. Pull tail of yarn through hole to inside of hat. Secure to WS.

FINISHING
Weave in ends. Mist hat with cool water and shape gently.

Chart

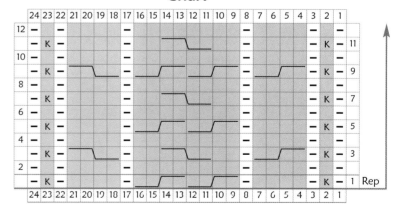

Key

▨	k on right side rows; p on wrong side rows.
—	p on right side rows; k on wrong side rows.
K	k into st below.
▱	sl 2 sts to cn and hold at back; k2; k2 from cn.
▰	sl 2 sts to cn and hold at front; k2; k2 from cn.

far country pullover

gregory courtney

MATERIALS

YARN: Jamieson's Shetland Chunky Marl (or Chunky Shetland) - 850 (950, 1,000) grams. Shown in Rainforest (2104).
NEEDLES: US 7 (4.5 mm) and US 9 (5.5 mm), ***or correct needles to obtain gauge.***
ACCESSORIES: Stitch holders.

MEASUREMENTS

CHEST: 43 (47, 51)".
LENGTH: 24 (25, 26)".
LENGTH TO ARMHOLE: 14 (14½, 15)".
ARMHOLE DEPTH: 10 (10½, 11)".
SLEEVE LENGTH: 20 (21, 22)".

GAUGE

On US 9 in **Reverse Waffle Stitch**: 16 sts and 22 rows = 4".

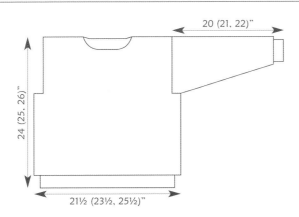

20 (21, 22)"

24 (25, 26)"

21½ (23½, 25½)"

CHART NOTES

Read odd-numbered (RS) rows from right to left and even-numbered (WS) rows from left to right. Although WS rows are charted, they can be worked as follows: ***knit the knit sts and purl the purl sts as they face you.*** Use instructions for **Reverse Waffle Stitch** (the background stitch of chart) when knitting gauge swatch and when knitting sleeves. Waist ribbing is included in chart to show smooth progression (and increases) from ribbing to body; however, it can be worked as **2x2 Rib**.

REVERSE WAFFLE STITCH (MULTIPLE OF 4 + 2)

Row 1 (RS): Purl.
Row 2 (WS): Knit.
Row 3 (RS): K2; *p2, k2; rep from *.
Row 4 (WS): P2; *k2, p2; rep from *.

Rep Rows 1-4.

2x2 RIB (MULTIPLE OF 4 + 2)

Row 1 (WS): P2; *k2, p2; rep from *.
Row 2 (RS): K2; *p2, k2; rep from *.

Rep Rows 1-2.

BACK

With US 7, CO 86 (94, 102) sts. Work the Foundation Row and Rows 1-14 of **Chart** *(or work 2x2 Rib)*, inc'g on Row 14 (WS) of **Chart** as shown *(or on 15th row (WS) if working 2x2 Rib)* (96 (104, 112) sts on needle). Change to US 9 and rep Rows 1-20 of **Chart** until piece measures 14 (14½, 15)" from CO edge, ending with RS facing for next row.

SHAPE ARMHOLES

BO 8 (8, 8) sts at beg of next 2 rows. Continue without further shaping on rem 80 (88, 96) sts until piece measures 23½ (24½, 25½)" from CO edge, ending with RS facing for next row.

SHAPE BACK NECK

Next Row (RS): Work 27 (31, 35) sts, BO next 26 (26, 26) sts, work 27 (31, 35) sts.

Turn, and working each side separately, dec 1 st at neck edge on next 2 rows. Place rem 25 (29, 33) shoulder sts on holders.

FRONT

Work same as for front until piece measures 20½ (21½, 22½)" from CO edge, ending with RS facing for next row.

SHAPE NECK

Next Row (RS): Work 33 (37, 41) sts, BO next 14 (14, 14) sts for front neck, work 33 (37, 41) sts.

Turn, and working each side separately, dec 1 st at neck edge on every RS row 8 (8, 8) times. Work without further shaping until piece measures same as back. Place rem 25 (29, 33) shoulder sts on holders.

JOIN SHOULDERS

Join shoulders using 3-needle bind-off method.

SLEEVES

With US 7, CO 34 (34, 34) sts. Work **2x2 Rib** for 15 rows, ending with RS facing for next row. Change to US 9, and work in **Reverse Waffle Stitch, AND AT SAME TIME,** inc 1 st at beg and end of 1st row once, then every 2nd Row 2 (2, 4) times, and every 4th row 19 (21, 21) times, working inc'd sts into pattern (78 (82, 86) sts on needle). Work without

further shaping until piece measures 20 (21, 22)" from CO edge. BO loosely.

NECKBAND

With US 7, RS facing, pick up 4 (4, 4) sts from right shoulder seam to back neck edge, 30 (30, 30) sts along back neck edge, 4 (4, 4) sts to left shoulder seam, 22 (22, 22) sts down left neck edge, 14 (14, 14) sts along front neck edge, and 22 (22, 22) sts up right neck edge (96 (96, 96) sts on needle). Join and work in the rnd as follows:

Every Rnd: *P2, k2; rep from *.

BO.

FINISHING

Center sleeves at shoulder seam and sew to body. Sew sleeve to BO edge at underarm. Sew sleeve and side seams. Weave in ends. Block to finished measurements.

Chart

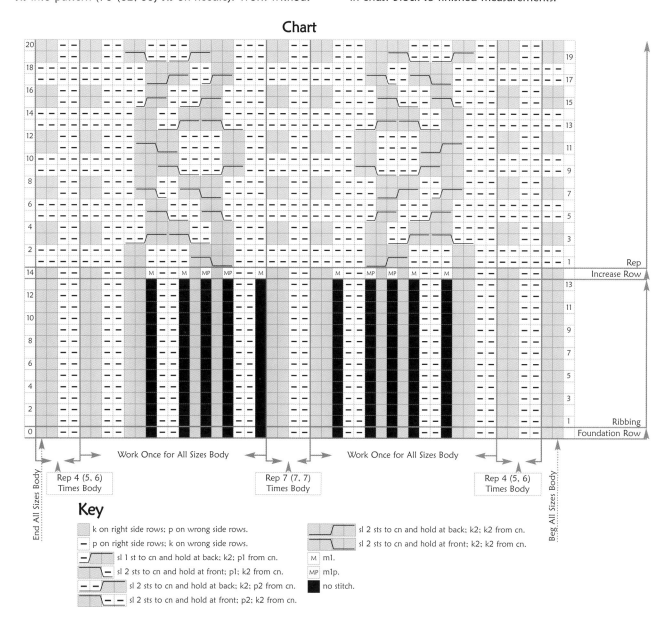

Key

	k on right side rows; p on wrong side rows.
−	p on right side rows; k on wrong side rows.
	sl 1 st to cn and hold at back; k2; p1 from cn.
	sl 2 sts to cn and hold at front; p1; k2 from cn.
	sl 2 sts to cn and hold at back; k2; p2 from cn.
	sl 2 sts to cn and hold at front; p2; k2 from cn.
	sl 2 sts to cn and hold at back; k2; k2 from cn.
	sl 2 sts to cn and hold at front; k2; k2 from cn.
M	m1.
MP	m1p.
■	no stitch.

camilla gloves

diane brown

MATERIALS

YARN: Jamieson's 2-Ply Shetland Spindrift - 75 (75) grams. Shown in Crimson (525).
NEEDLES: Set of 4 double-pointed and 24" circular US 1 (2.50 mm) and set of 4 double-pointed US 2 (3 mm), *or correct needles to obtain gauge.*
ACCESSORIES: Stitch holders or waste yarn. Tapestry needle.

MEASUREMENTS

LENGTH (MEASURED FROM CO EDGE TO TIP OF MIDDLE FINGER): 10 (10½)".
CIRCUMFERENCE AT PALM: 6½ (7¼)".

GAUGE

On US 2 in st st: 32 sts and 40 rows = 4".

Chart

18	−	⌐	−	⌐	−	⌐	−	⌐	O	/	18
17	−	⌐	−	⌐	−	⌐	−	O	⌐	/	17
16	−	⌐	−	⌐	−	⌐	O	⌐	−	/	16
15	−	⌐	−	⌐	−	O	⌐	−	⌐	/	15
14	−	⌐	−	⌐	O	⌐	−	⌐	−	/	14
13	−	⌐	−	O	⌐	−	⌐	−	⌐	/	13
12	−	⌐	O	⌐	−	⌐	−	⌐	−	/	12
11	−	O	⌐	−	⌐	−	⌐	−	⌐	/	11
10	O	⌐	−	⌐	−	⌐	−	⌐	−	/	10
9	/	−	⌐	−	⌐	−	⌐	−	⌐	O	9
8	⌐	/	−	⌐	−	⌐	−	⌐	−	O	8
7	⌐	−	/	−	⌐	−	⌐	−	⌐	O	7
6	⌐	−	⌐	/	−	⌐	−	⌐	−	O	6
5	⌐	−	⌐	−	/	−	⌐	−	⌐	O	5
4	⌐	−	⌐	−	⌐	/	−	⌐	−	O	4
3	⌐	−	⌐	−	⌐	−	/	−	⌐	O	3
2	⌐	−	⌐	−	⌐	−	⌐	/	−	O	2
1	⌐	−	⌐	−	⌐	−	⌐	−	/	O	1

→ Rep 8 (8) Times ←

Key

⌐	ktbl.
−	p.
/	k2togtbl.
O	yo.

DESIGNER NOTE

To customize finger length to fit wearer, knit to middle of fingernail, then work **Dec and Close Fingertip** instructions.

NOTES ON CHART

As gloves are knitted entirely in the rnd, read all rows from right to left.

PICOT CAST-ON

*CO 4 sts, BO 2 sts, place last st back on left-hand needle; rep from * until desired number of sts are cast on.

2X2 RIB (MULTIPLE OF 4)

Every Rnd: *K2, p2; rep from *.

EYELET PATTERN

Rnd 1: Purl.
Rnd 2: *K2tog, yo; rep from * to end.
Rnd 3: Knit.
Rnd 4: Purl.

GLOVES

CUFF

With 24" circular US 1, CO 80 (80) sts using **Picot Cast-On**. Knit 1 row. Distribute sts onto three US 2 double-pointed needles, place marker for beg of rnd and join. Work the 18 rnds of **Chart**. Knit 2 rnds, dec'g 28 (24) sts evenly spaced on 2nd rnd (52 (56) sts on needles). Change to US 1 and work 6 rnds in **2X2 Rib**. Work **Eyelet Pattern**. Work 6 rnds in **2X2 Rib**, inc'g 1 st at end of 6th rnd (53 (57) sts on needles).

PALM AND THUMB GUSSET

K25 (27) sts, place marker, m1, k3, m1, place marker, knit to end of rnd. Knit 2 rnds. Rep incs every 3rd rnd after 1st and before 2nd markers until there are 19 (21) thumb gusset sts between markers. Knit 3 rnds.

Next rnd: Knit to 1st marker and remove it. Place thumb gusset sts on holder, remove 2nd marker, CO 4 (4) sts to bridge gap between palm and back of hand, knit 25 (27) sts. Work in st st until palm measures 3¼ (3¾)".

LITTLE FINGER

K6 (7) sts, place 42 (44) sts on holder, CO 4 (4) sts, knit to end of rnd (16 (18) sts on needles). Working on 3 needles, knit until finger measures 2 (2¼)".

DEC AND CLOSE FINGERTIP

Dec Rnd 1: *K2tog; rep from *.
Next Rnd: Knit.
Dec Rnd 2: *K2tog; rep from *.

Break yarn, thread onto darning needle, draw through rem sts, push through hole to inside. pull tight to close and weave in end.

RING FINGER

Holding glove with little finger at right, k6 (7) sts from holder, CO 4 (4) sts, k6 (7) sts from holder, pick up 4 (4) sts from base of little finger (20 (22) sts on needles). Knit 1 rnd. On next rnd, knit 15 (17) sts, k2tog, k1, k2tog (2 sts dec'd). Work until finger measures 2¼ (2½)". **Dec and Close Fingertip** same as for little finger.

MIDDLE FINGER

Holding glove with little finger at right, k7 (7) sts from holder, CO 2 (4) sts, k7 (7) sts from holder, pick up 4 (4) sts at base of ring finger (20 (22) sts on needles). Work 1 rnd. Dec 2 sts on next rnd as in ring finger (18 (20) sts on needles). Work until finger measures 2½ (2¾)". **Dec and Close Fingertip** same as for little finger.

INDEX FINGER

Knit rem 16 (16) sts, pick up 2 (4) sts at base of middle finger (18 (20) sts on needles). Work without dec'g until finger measures 2¼ (2½)". **Dec and Close Fingertip** same as for little finger.

THUMB

K19 (21) sts of thumb gusset, pick up 3 (3) sts from side of palm below index finger. Knit 1 rnd. On next rnd, dec 2 sts on inside of thumb (20 (22) sts on needles). Work until thumb measures 1¾ (2)". **Dec and Close Fingertip** same as for little finger.

BOW

With US 1 circular, CO 155 sts. BO all sts. Weave in ends. Thread through eyelet holes at wrist, and make small knot at each end of cord. Tie in a bow. *Be sure to position bow on back of wrist for each hand.*

FINISHING

Weave in ends (use ends to close gaps at base of fingers, if necessary). Join yarn at picot edge, aligning picots along edge. Block gently.

Abbreviations

alt = alternate
beg = beginning
BO = bind off
CC = contrast color
cn = cable needle
CO = cast on
dec = decrease(ing)
foll = follow(ing)
GS = garter stitch
inc = increase(ing)
k = knit
kfb = knit into front and back of st (inc)
k1b = knit through back loop
k2tog = knit 2 sts together
k2togtbl = knit 2 sts together through back loop
m1 = make 1 st (inc) - lift running thread between st just worked and next st and knit into back of loop
m1p = make 1 st (inc) purl - lift running thread between st just worked and next st and purl into front of loop
kwise = knitwise (as if to knit)
MC = main color
p = purl
p2tog = purl 2 sts together
patt = pattern
psp = p1 and slip to left-hand needle; pass next st over it; return to right-hand needle
psso = pass slipped st over st just knitted
p2sso = pass 2 slipped sts over st just knitted
p3sso = pass 3 slipped sts over st just knitted
pwise - purlwise (as if to purl)
rem = remaining
rep = repeat
rnd = round
RS = right side
sl = slip
sl1wyib = with yarn in back, slip 1 st pwise
sl1wyif = with yarn in front, slip 1 st pwise
ssk = sl 2 sts (one at a time) kwise; with left-hand needle, knit these two sts tog through front of sts
ssp = sl 2 sts kwise (one at a time); return both sts to left-hand needle; k2togtbl
st(s) = stitch(es)
st st = stockinette stitch
tbl = through back loop
tog = together
WS = wrong side
yo = (inc) yarn over needle

Skill Levels

Beginner    *Intermediate*    *Expert*

*Jamieson's Shetland wool is distributed in North America by **Simply** Shetland and can be found at these fine stores:*

CALIFORNIA
Los Altos
Uncommon Threads
650-941-1815
www.uncommonthreadsyarn.com

Mendocino
Mendocino Yarn Shop
888-530-1400
www.mendocinoyarnshop.com

Oakland
Article Pract
510-652-7435
www.articlepract.com

The Knitting Basket
510-339-6295
www.theknittingbasket.com

Pacific Grove
Monarch Knitting & Quilts
831-657-9276
www.monarchknitting.com

Sebastopol
Knitting Workshop
707-824-0699

COLORADO
Colorado Springs
Needleworks by Holly Berry
719-636-1002
www.hollyberryhouse.com

CONNECTICUT
Avon
Wool Connection
860-678-1710
www.woolconnection.com

Chaplin
Yarns with a Twist
860-455-9986

Glastonbury
Village Wool
860-633-0898

Deep River
Yarns Down Under
860-526-9986
www.yarnsdownunder.com

Mystic
Mystic River Yarns
860-536-4305

New Preston
The Village Sheep, LLC
860-354-5442

Newington
Needleworks
800-665-0277
www.needleworksonline.com

Stratford
Janet Kemp, LLC
203-386-9276
www.janetkemp.com

Woodbridge
The Yarn Barn
203-389-5117
www.theyarnbarn.com

GEORGIA
Roswell
Cast-On Cottage
770-998-3483

ILLINOIS
Des Plaines
Mosaic Yarn Studio, Ltd.
847-390-1013
www.mosaicyarnstudio.com

Lake Forest
The Keweenaw Shepherd
847-295-9524

INDIANA
Fort Wayne
Cass Street Depot
888-420-2292
www.cassstreetdepot.com

Valparaiso
Sheep's Clothing
219-462-1700

MAINE
Camden
Stitchery Square
207-236-9773
www.stitcherysquare.com

MARYLAND
Bethesda
Yarns International
800-927-6728
www.yarnsinternational.com

Columbia
All About Yarn
410-992-5648

MASSACHUSETTS
Brookfield
KnitWitts
877-877-KNIT
www.knitwitts.com

Brookline
A Good Yarn
617-731-4900
www.agoodyarn.biz

Cambridge
Woolcott & Company
617-547-2837
www.woolcottandco.com

Cohasett
Creative Stitch
781-383-0667

Hyannis
Blue Heron Yarn Studio
508-775-5663
www.blueheronyarn.com

Lenox
Colorful Stitches
800-413-6111
www.colorful-stitches.com

Lexington
Wild & Woolly Studio
781-861-7717
wwoolly@aol.com

Northampton
Northampton Wools
413-586-4331

Plymouth
Knitting Treasures
508-747-2500

South Hamilton
Cranberry Fiber Arts
978-468-3871
www.cranberryfiberarts.com

Vineyard Haven
Heath Hen Quilt Shop
508-693-6730
www.heathhen.com

MICHIGAN
Ada
Clever Ewe
616-682-1545

Berkley
Have You Any Wool
248-541-9665

Birmingham
Knitting Room
248-540-3623
www.knittingroom.com

Grosse Point
The Wool & the Floss, Ltd
313-882-9110
www.thewoolandthefloss.com

Lake Orion
Heritage Spinning & Weaving
248-693-3690
www.heritagespinning.com

Marquette
Town Folk Gallery
906-225-9010
www.townfolkgallery.com

Rochester
Skeins on Main
248-656-9300
www.skeinsonmain.com

Tawas Bay
Tawas Bay Yarn Company
989-362-4463

MINNESOTA
Duluth
Yarn Harbor
218-724-6432
www.yarnharbor.com

Maple Grove
Yarn Cafe
763-478-2899

Minneapolis
Linden Hills Yarns
612-929-1255

Needlework Unlimited
888-925-2454
www.needleworkunlimited.com

Skeins
952-939-4166

St. Paul
Borealis Yarns
651-646-2488
www.borealisyarns.com

Three Kittens Yarn Shoppe
651-457-4969

The Yarnery
651-222-5793

White Bear Lake
A Sheepy Yarn Shoppe
800-480-5462
www.sheepyyarn.com

MONTANA
Calispell
Woolen Collectibles
406-756-8746

NEW HAMPSHIRE
Exeter
Charlotte's Web
603-778-1417
www.charlotteswebyarns.com

Laconia
The Yarn Shop & Fibres
603-528-1221
www.yarnshoponline.com

NEW JERSEY
Princeton
Pins and Needles
609-921-9075
www.pinsandneedles.biz

NEW MEXICO
Albuquerque
Village Wools, Inc.
505-883-2919
www.villagewools.com

NEW YORK
Locust Valley
All About Ewe
516-609-3002
www.allaboutewe.com

Rochester
Spirit Works Knitting & Design
585-544-9107

OHIO
Columbus
Knitter's Mercantile
614-888-8551
www.knittersmercantile.com

Toledo
FiberWorks Knitting & Weaving
419-389-1821

OKLAHOMA
Tulsa
Naturally Needlepoint & Knitting
918-747-8838

OREGON
Ashland
The Web-sters
800-482-9801
www.yarnatwebsters.com

Carlton
Woodland Woolworks
800-547-3725
www.woolworks.com

Eugene
The Knit Shop
541-434-0430
www.knit-shop.com

Pacific City
Nestucca Bay Textile & Supply
877-401-1528

Portland
Knit Purl
503-227-2999
www.knit-purl.com

PENNSYLVANIA
Chambersburg
The Yarn Basket
888-976-2758
www.yarnbasketpa.com

Kennett Square
Wool Gathering
610-444-8236
www.woolgathering.com

Lancaster
Oh Susanna
717-393-5146

Philadelphia
Rosie's Yarn Cellar
215-977-9276
www.rosiesyarncellar.com

Tangled Web
215-242-1271
www.tangledwebb.com

RHODE ISLAND
Pawtucket
Yarns At Lace Wings
401-475-7500
www.yarnsatlacewings.com

Providence
A Stitch Above
800-949-5648
www.knitri.com

Wickford
And the Beads Go On...
401-268-3899

UTAH
Sandy
Unraveled Sheep
801-255-6833

VIRGINIA
Burke
The Yarn Barn
800-762-5274
www.geocities.com/theyarnbarnonline

Dillwyn
Yarn Barn of Andersonville
800-850-6008
www.yarnbarn.com

Richmond
Lettuce Knit
804-323-5777

WASHINGTON
Bainbridge Island
Churchmouse Yarns & Teas
206-780-2686
www.churchmouseyarns.com

Kent
The Two Swans Yarns
888-830-8269
www.twoswansyarns.com

Port Angeles
A Mingled Yarn
360-457-0133
www.amingledyarn.com

Renton
Knittery
800-742-3565

Seattle
So Much Yarn...
800-443-0727
www.somuchyarn.com

The Weaving Works
888-524-1221
www.weavingworks.com

WISCONSIN
Appleton
Jane's Knitting Hutch
920-954-9001
www.janesknittinghutch.com

Delafield
The Knitting Ark
262-646-2464

Madison
Lakeside Fibers
608-257-2999
www.lakesidefibers.com

Milwaukee
Ruhama's Yarn & Needlepoint
414-332-2660
www.ruhamas.com

Neenah
Yarns by Design
888-559-2767
www.yarnsbydesign.com

Verona
Sow's Ear
608-848-2755
www.knitandsip.com

CANADA/Ontario
Ancaster
The Needle Emporium
905-648-1994
www.needleemporium.com

Kingston
The Wool Room
800-449-5868 (in Canada)
613-544-9544
info@woolroom.on.ca

Orangeville
Camilla Valley Farm
519-941-0736
www.camillavalleyfarm.com

Toronto
Four Seasons Knitting Products
888-388-6848
www.fourseasonsknitting.com

Toronto
She Ewe Knits
905-878-7990
www.sheeweknits.com

A very special thanks to Milo Shepard, great nephew and trustee of the Jack London estate, for allowing this book to be photographed at his beautiful home, the Jack London Ranch and Vineyard, Glen Ellen, California.

Editorial Director   **David Codling**

Editor & Graphic Design   **Gregory Courtney**

Photography   **Kathryn Martin**

Illustrations   **Molly Eckler**

Garments Modeled by   **Michelle Rich, Nate Barker, Grace Eckler, Jack Thornton, Virgnia Hunter & "Leo"**

Makeup & Hair Styling   **Kira Lee**

Clothing Stylist   **Betsy Westman**

Buttons   **Muench Buttons**   www.muenchyarns.com

Location Thanks   **Milo Shepard, Jack London Vineyard, Glen Ellen, California**

Location Coordinator   **Betty Lou Bond**

A Very Special Thanks   **Neil Shepard, *Country Carriage Charter*, Clydesdales**

Color Reproduction & Printing   **Regent Publishing Services, Ltd.**

Jamieson's Shetland Wools Distributed in North America By   **Simply Shetland**   www.simplyshetland.net

Jamieson's Shetland Wools Distributed in Europe By   **Jamieson's Spinning, Ltd.**   www.jamiesonsofshetland.co.uk

Published and Distributed By   **Unicorn Books and Crafts, Inc.**   www.unicornbooks.com

Printed in China

ISBN
1-893063-12-7

1 2 3 4 5 6 7 8 9 10